# A CHURCH AT RISK

# A CHURCH AT RISK

*The Challenge of
Spiritually
Hungry Adults*

MARCEL J. DUMESTRE

*A Crossroad Herder Book*
The Crossroad Publishing Company
New York

1997

The Crossroad Publishing Company
370 Lexington Avenue, New York, NY 10017

Printed in the United States of America

### Library of Congress Cataloguing-in-Publication Data

Dumestre, Marcel J.
    A church at risk  :   the challenge of spiritually hungry adults   /
Marcel J. Dumestre.
        p.   cm.
    Parts of the manuscript appeared in articles written by the author
from 1991–1995.
    Includes bibliographical references.
    ISBN 0-8245-1461-0 (pbk.)
        1. Spirituality—United States.   2. United States—Religion—1960-
3. Humanism, Religious.   I. Title.
BV4501.2.D747   1997
277.3'0829—dc21                                                97-4143
                                                                    CIP

# CONTENTS

92255

*To Margie and Robin*

# FOREWORD

The completion of a book is an interesting process. As one concludes final editing, the many influences that went into the construction of the manuscript become all the more apparent. This book is
no different.

I am indebted particularly to Michael Leach, publisher of Cross-
road/Herder Publishing Company, for his encouragement and ex-
citement about this book from its very beginning to its long overdue
completion. Sr. Mary Margaret Doorley, Crossroad national consultant, also supported this project with her unbridled optimism and
dream for church communities to be responsive to adult spirituality.
Closer to home, Barbara J. Fleischer, associate professor of practical theology at Loyola University New Orleans, kindly provided an
insightful critique of manuscript drafts. Katherine Alito, resident gram-
marian, provided excellent corrections to the first draft. I also owe a
debt of gratitude to manuscript editor Joan Marie Laflamme for her
keen eye and insight. She did an embarrassingly wonderful job editing the manuscript.

It was not until the completion of this book that I realized how I
have been influenced by the work of Robert O'Gorman, Jack
Seymour, and Charles R. Foster. These scholarly leaders in the field
of religious education in large part forged the grand experiment in
doctoral religious education at Scarritt Theological Graduate School
and Vanderbilt University. I thank them for what might have been,
their courage of conviction, and ongoing dedication to the field.

This book has been a work in progress for quite some time. Parts
of the manuscript appeared in articles that I wrote for the following
publications. "Post-Fundamentalism and the Christian Intentional
Learning Community," *Religious Education* 90 (Spring 1995), 190–
206; "Beyond Fundamentalism: Adult Religious Education for Adult
Spirituality," *Catholic World* (September/October 1994), 219–225;
"The Preferential Option for Adults, Part One: A Church at Risk,"
*PACE* 23 (April 1994), 20–25; "The Preferential Option for Adults,
Part Two: Educating Leaders in a New Paradigm," *PACE* 23 (May
1994), 14–18; "Toward Effective Adult Religious Education,"

*Origins* 23(2) (May 27, 1993), 24–28; "Finding Unity in Diversity in Church-Related Higher Education: Four Conceptual Principles," *Religious Education* 87 (Fall 1992), 587–605; "Liberal Arts Education as an Expression of Religious Education: Higher Education for a Pluralistic Society," *Religious Education* 86 (Spring 1991), 292–306; "Understanding Traditionalism," InFormation 4 (November 1996), 4–7.

# INTRODUCTION

This book is written for "We the People of the United States" who do not attend church regularly and perhaps even have forgotten why. It also is intended for those of us who attend every week out of a sense of duty but find little meaning and worry about religion's relevance to a spiritually hungry U.S. culture. Most important, this book is written for ministers and religious educators who want to meet the needs of all Christians who seek deeper meaning in life and long for the religion of their childhood to make sense to them as adults.

We have a crisis of religion in the United States, but not a crisis of faith. Gallup polls over the last half of this century suggest that adults today are just as spiritual as they have ever been. The problem, however, is that many adults are distrustful of religion. Tele-evangelist scandals, pedophilia cases, and other exposés have taken their toll, but there are even deeper problems. The typical Christian theology preached from Christian church pulpits tends not to make sense to many adults. Too many sermons consist of worn-out religious platitudes that do not address the complexity of contemporary life situations. Likewise, too many Christian adult religious education programs remain unattractive to adults, which means that the typical adult Christian relies upon the inadequate conceptions of religion they learned in childhood. The typical adult Christian today is trying to make sense out of the ultimate questions of life with a childhood base of religious knowledge. In this sense, Christianity is failing the American people, which places Christianity as a church at risk.

Not all Christian churches are losing membership, however. Fundamentalist churches that present Christianity as a simple, straightforward expression of a literal interpretation of the Bible are flourishing today. While fundamentalist churches are growing, mainline Christian churches are losing membership. In the same vein as tele-evangelism, fundamentalist churches present simple answers to complex religious questions. This is a very attractive approach to religion, but, in the long run, it does not lead to mature spirituality. Moreover, it does not have the confidence of the majority of American Christians.

Mainline Christianity is caught today in between embracing a deceptively simple fundamentalistic approach to religion and an intellectual approach that is far too complex. The tendency of many mainline churches is to emulate fundamentalism's uncomplicated approach to religion in order to maintain and attract membership. Indeed, the uncertainties of the late twentieth century make fundamentalism's proclamations of absolute certainty an attractive commodity. The body of Christian theological reflection over the past fifty years, however, indicates that absolute certainty is not so easily attainable, if attainable at all. Responsibly trusting in the gracious goodness of a mysterious God is closer to the theological mainstream. But the theological scholarship that leads to such conclusions is inaccessible (and uninteresting) to most adult Christians. How then can mainstream Christianity avoid both a fundamentalistic and an overly intellectual approach to theology and church life? This book offers an answer. The following guide through the chapters offers a rationale for the construction of such an answer.

### 1. *Awakenings*

Stories are the heart of this book. Almost all of the chapters begin with stories of real-life situations. Chapter 1 starts with stories of spiritual awakenings. These stories present critical moments in which ultimate questions of life are raised and how Christian churches were unable to adequately address those questions. The book's central message is articulated, namely, that the central purpose of Christianity is the promotion of mature spirituality. Too often one gets the impression that institutional self-promotion is the primary purpose of religion. A key element to enabling mature spirituality is fostering religious literacy that empowers and enables adults to make religious sense out of their everyday lives. Religious literacy, in this vein, does not mean learning religious facts simply for the sake of it. Rather, it means acquiring a working knowledge of the ongoing Christian story, warts and all, in order to give wider meaning to one's own life story. To be religiously literate is to be empowered in the most important dimension of one's life. To be religiously illiterate is to be disempowered.

### 2. *Religiosity in American Life*

Chapter 2 builds upon the awakening stories with sociological and poll data indicating the need for spirituality in a broader sense. We are not alone in our individual stories, as much as that might seem to be the case during moments of crisis. Moreover, it is comforting to know that we are not alone in our quest for meaning. Sociologists and developmental psychologists suggest there are common themes to this seemingly solitary quest. Different models of religiosity in the United States are explored, as well as different stages of religious affiliation.

This chapter also presents James Fowler's contention that faith is a natural part of the human constitution. He suggests that faith helps us form a dependable "life space," an environment in which the ultimate questions of life can be addressed. It is the function of religion to help us landscape that environment. Fowler also gives us a framework with his articulation of stages of faith to situate our own faith journey toward mature spirituality.

### 3. A Fundamentalist World View

Chapter 3 presents the primary features of the dominant religious world view in U.S. Christianity today—fundamentalism. Origins of fundamentalism are discussed along with its basic tenets. Two primary points are made in the chapter. First, fundamentalism is much more pervasive in Christianity than the formal churches and movements that name themselves as fundamentalist. Fundamentalism can be described as a religious world view that pervades all Christian churches and, indeed, all of the major world religions. The most difficult aspect of this world view, as with all extreme positions, is that it tends to impede the development of a mature spirituality.

The second primary point of the chapter is that, despite claims to the contrary, fundamentalism is very different than conservatism. Christianity needs conservatives and liberals, and every position in between. The problem lies with radicals on both the religious right and the religious left. While this book deals with the outlying world view on the right, I acknowledge problems with the radical left and leave that problem for other critics. Most important, radical world views keep Christianity honest and vibrant. As painful as it may be, the radicals force those of us in the (maybe too comfortable) middle to affirm what is good and effective and to jettison that which is less than good and ineffective.

### 4. Christian Spiritual Humanism

Chapter 4 offers an answer to a fundamentalistic religious world view—Christian spiritual humanism. This alternative world view recognizes the very real human needs that fundamentalism satisfies and offers a potentially more growthful alternative. The book pivots on this short chapter. The preceding chapters make the case for

Christianity as a church at risk. This chapter offers a conceptual framework for approaching the ultimate questions of life that resonates with the cultural situation of late twentieth century U.S. culture in which We the People find ourselves. The chapters that follow offer ways of implementing this religious world view in the life of Christian institutions.

### 5. *Education of the Public*

Chapter 5 reflects on the value-laden aspects of education in the United States. Americans have placed their trust in the power of public education to create a better world. This mandate is spiritually charged despite the rhetoric about value-free or value-neutral education. Education cannot be anything but value laden.

Four primary points are made in the chapter. First, education of the public is not confined to schooling. There is an ecology of institutions in society that educate—mass media, church, family, government, and so forth. The totality of these educational influences form the *paiedia* —a culture's self-understanding. Second, it is important to recognize the proximate and ultimate aims of education. Proximately, people are educated for the arts, crafts, careers, and professions. The ultimate aims of education enter the realm of spirituality. Are we educating people for the common good, or for emancipation, or for self-actualization, or for other ends? Third, there is a need for public conversation about the ultimate aims of education. No doubt, there are conflicting values at the heart of different educational institutions. Can there be consensus on the ultimate aims of education? Fourth, public educators and Christian religious educators should have the same ultimate goal—growth. One might ask, "Growth toward what?" The public educator might answer, "Growth in human potential." The Christian religious educator might answer, "Transcendence." It is proposed that Christian religious educators need to be part of the great cultural conversation on the ultimate aims of education. Instead of calling for prayer in schools, Christian educators should be educating children and adults on how interpret and evaluate the conflicting values that are part of the U.S. educational ecology. The next chapter gives a way for this type of education to take place.

### 6. *Spiritual Education*

This chapter proposes that Christian religious education be reconceptualized as spiritual education for the purpose of actualizing Christian spiritual humanism in church and community life.

Spiritual education is described as intentional meaning-making and value-laden learning that encompasses five interrelated realities: critical consciousness, authentic community, prophetic action, institutional identity, and spiritual growth. If any one of these elements is missing, then such education is something other than spiritual education. The theoretical foundations of spiritual education are unpacked in the chapter, and possibilities are explored for the positive influence of church education on the popular culture.

## 7. Spiritual Higher Education

Poll data tend to indicate an inverse relationship between level of education and levels of religiosity. The more one is educated the less likely he or she is to be religious. Why is this the case? This chapter explores that question. Critics of higher education claim that colleges and universities today have lost the moral rudder of their denominational beginnings in the United States. The tenets of spiritual education are applied to the context of higher education.

The chapter also presents a reflection on how church-related higher education can use the principles of spiritual education as a guide for academic and administrative policy. The specific situation of Catholic colleges and universities is taken as a case in point. The recent debate on the interplay of Catholic church magisterial authority and university autonomy is a good instance of how spiritual education can help people of good will negotiate potentially troubled waters.

## 8. A Church at Risk

This last chapter begins with a story about how Christian spiritual humanism can be implemented in Christian congregational life. The chapter presents a summary of why Christianity is a church at risk in the United States. It brings together the argument for Christian spiritual humanism as a religious world view that can successfully counter the current dominance of fundamentalism in U.S. Christianity. The importance of spiritual education in the life of Christian parishes and congregations is explored. Implications for how Christian churches might better meet the spiritual needs of U.S. Christian adults are outlined as "Lessons for the Churches." The concluding section presents a story about a dream that captures the spirit of what is being conveyed in this volume.

This book offers only one perspective on a deep-seated and complex religious and cultural problem. Much more is left out than included. Even though prayer and more aesthetic dimensions of religion and spirituality are immensely important, I concentrate on religious education in this book. My experience and education compel me to do so. Moreover, I believe that grappling with the ultimate questions of life, with the resources and stories of those who have come before us, makes possible a better life for ourselves. I invite you to find yourself in the stories that follow.

# Chapter 1

# AWAKENINGS

My mother-in-law died when my wife and I were in our early thirties. She left this world quietly at her home in Miami. We were at least comforted by that, since she hated hospitals so much. She was not a recent transplant to Miami from the north. She and her husband moved to Miami in the 1940s—the pioneer's Miami, as her friends would often say. My father-in-law gave up his career as a South Dakota barnstorming pilot to move to Miami. One of my wife's proudest possessions is a picture of her father sitting in an open-air cockpit in a brown leather flight jacket and a leather helmet with a white scarf wrapped around his neck. The smile on his wrinkled face gives the impression that he was about to say, "Yes, I'm the real thing."

Their move to Miami meant a move from the cockpit to the ground as a mechanic. He built his own house and a rental unit in the backyard—the insurance policy of his generation. He died of a heart attack in his living room when my wife was in her teens. His heart attack was almost twenty years before my mother-in-law's death. She died in the living room as well. A quick and peaceful death, we were told. It was hard to tell whether it was the truth or we were just being consoled. Her death, in that respect, was like her life. She was a quiet, sensitive woman who tended to worry a lot about things over which she had no control. There was a childlike quality about her; she tended to be completely accepting of other people. But she was fiercely independent and lived life according to her own terms.

The death of a loved one has a way of slowing down time and making room for thoughts and conversations that are submerged by the busyness of everyday life. It was that way for us. The long silences on the flight to Miami were interspersed with the calmness of those heartfelt conversations that, after the fact, we wonder why we did not have more often. The funeral was a traditional affair, with one exceptional moment.

I can remember kneeling at the side of my mother-in-law's coffin—an expensive one that she would never have bought for herself—when my wife turned to me and asked, "Where is she, really?" We both fell silent. All of the Christian religious education of our lives lay before us. The answers from the catechism of our childhood came quickly to mind. Now, as adults, however, we took pause. We believed that she was with God, but what does that really mean for us as adults? This question amounted to a faith crisis—an awakening to the need to be honest about our faith. We could not embrace the simplistic religious answers of our childhood. Sunday after Sunday we heard a lot about heaven and hell, but we seldom heard anything that came close to addressing the substance of our questions. We felt a stronger need for spirituality in our lives, yet our religion seemed to be increasingly less relevant. We did not know what was happening to us.

We stopped going to church for a while. Why did we not bring our problems to our pastor, we asked ourselves. We were afraid; we blamed ourselves for not being able to find meaning in Sunday services. We thought that we were the problem. If services were not meaningful, then there was something wrong with us. We just plain felt guilty. Our religion was very important to us as children and adolescents. We followed the rules. What did we do so wrong that, now as adults, we started doubting the most basic elements of our religious beliefs? We started a circuitous and rather fumbling search for answers to our questions that ended up with a return to church life, but a return to a conception of church that was vastly different from the church of our childhood.

At about the same time our friends Bill and Kathy[1] were expecting their second child. Bill is an engineer and Kathy is college educated as well, but she preferred not to work outside the home and sold her crafts at area flea markets in her spare time. Bill and Kathy were children of the 1960s. Their style of clothing was different from what they wore in the 1960s, and their hair was cut to the style of the day. But attitudinally, they were still flower children.

Bill and Kathy had experimented with drugs in college and probably still used marijuana occasionally. They had had a traditional Catholic upbringing, but had not attended church much since their high school days. They felt that they were missing something spiritual in their lives and tried attending the local Catholic church. But it did not work for them.

Through the encouragement of friends they tried attending services held by a preacher at a large local motel. The preacher had an amazing ability to attract people who were troubled and searching for something in which to believe. The congregation was a composite of society—young and old, educated and uneducated, wealthy and poor. A common thread that brought them together was pain. They all were hurting. Some were trying to make sense of why they were sick, others had trouble with their marriages or their children, and still others had a deep anxiety they could not quite verbalize. The minority that did not pray for some sort of healing attended out of certainty that the unadulterated fire and brimstone of hell needed to be preached in order to get back to the basic values that made this country great.

Bill and Kathy described the preacher as man of slight build, penetrating eyes, and a voice deeper than his physique seemed to allow. He had the ability to take a passage from the Bible and somehow make it speak to everyone in attendance.

The services were simple and direct. An upright piano played by the preacher's wife provided music for rhythmic hymns that he would start spontaneously during his sermons. Our friends declared that they had given up all of their vices and proclaimed themselves "saved by the blood of Christ." Bill and Kathy pored over the Bible and became closer to the community that formed around the services held every Sunday. A local church building was being planned. As they put it, "God replaced the drugs in our lives."

My wife and I were happy for them at first. But as time went on, we became troubled by their increasingly hostile attitude toward society. A month before the delivery of their baby Bill and Kathy announced that they believed that God's will would guide the birth of their child, not modern medicine and drugs. The baby would be delivered at home with the help of some of the church women. The women's sole function was to pray during the delivery; they possessed no midwifery skills. The baby was delivered with complications; Bill panicked and called 911. Help arrived, and Kathy and the baby were eventually saved after a hospital stay.

Bill and Kathy were devastated. They were educated people, but their church placed their zeal for spirituality in contradiction with their sense of appropriate medical care. Kathy and their baby were almost lost in the process. Their whole world was thrown into chaos at a time that should have been filled with joy and happiness. In their minds, religion had failed them.

A few years later we met Laura, an accountant with an abiding interest in the spiritual side of life. She grew up Presbyterian, but left the church in her thirties after her divorce. She earned an advanced degree and began her own accounting practice. Shortly after she opened the business, she started experimenting with different types of human development programs and New Age spirituality groups. She said that the groups helped her overcome the fear of failure. My wife and I attended some introductory sessions with Laura. I was somewhat taken by what was said in the meetings: the importance of self-awareness, the potential of overcoming deep-seated fears, honesty with oneself and others, discovering the potential of human existence, and finding God within ourselves. My wife was less comfortable. She noticed a "knowing" attitude among the group members, who talked about not having all of the answers to life's questions but acted as if they did. The meetings were held in comfortable surroundings with all of the trappings of peace and solace. Group members were genuinely searching for how to be more loving, but we did not feel comfortable with them.

Laura always had been a searcher for religious meaning in her life, but her search intensified when she was diagnosed with a life-threatening blood disease. She was on a quest for religious answers among nontraditional forms of religion. Laura was adamant about not exploring the religion of her childhood. She had long ago written off mainline Christian religion as hopelessly bound up with patriarchal authority and organization and unable to address the concerns of a new age. There also was an incident that occurred in her twenties,when she was totally devoted to her church, that devastated her and to which she only obliquely referred when talking about traditional religion as irrelevant and hypocritical.

My wife and I still visit Laura. She tells us about the newest discoveries in her spiritual life and developments in New Age religious movements. She seems genuinely happy. Laura asks about our lives and about our daughter. She also inquires in a polite but somewhat uneasy way about the latest trends in mainline Christianity. As I drive away from our visits with her, I always feel a sense of loss and worry about her health, the solitariness of her life, and the transitory nature of religious experimentalism. I also feel a sadness about what might have been if Laura had felt that there was room for her in the religion of her childhood.

Angelle, another friend, taught philosophy at a local university and was a deeply religious person. She was raised Catholic, but she left the church early in her graduate studies. The rigid categories of Neo-Scholastic philosophy that she learned in her undergraduate studies at a Catholic university in the 1950s fell apart as she was introduced to other schools of philosophical thought in her doctoral studies. Metaphysics was her life.

Squarely in the midst of her agnosticism, when God was purely a concept to be studied, Angelle experienced a conversion in a most unusual way—she bought a dog. Initially she bought the dog for protection. Duke was a stocky puppy with an expressive face who, within two years, would grow to be a powerful and protective boxer. She soon found that Duke needed a lot attention, including walks in the morning and evening. At first Angelle tolerated the walks in the park. But she lived in the world of concepts and had little patience for walking and waiting for Duke to relieve himself over and over again. Duke, on the other hand, was in no hurry to get back to the house.

Over the course of a year, however, Angelle came to enjoy their jaunts in the park. Quite unexpectedly she caught herself praying during one of their walks. She did not know where it came from or how it happened, but she was praying nonetheless. Prior to that moment, prayer had involved making deals with God to get what she wanted. Most of us are all too familiar with such deals. But now Angelle was praying, talking to God, out of sheer love and gratitude for having Duke in her life. It was Duke and the beauty of the trees, flowers, and stream in the park that enabled her to see the God that metaphysics never revealed.

She continued praying during her walks and came to know God for the first time. As she reflected upon her religious upbringing, it seemed that she was far too busy *learning about* God rather coming to *know* God. She was cautious at first about telling friends of her experience. When she did, they seemed supportive, but most people did not quite understand the intensity of her experience.

Angelle decided to talk about her prayer life with a young, newly ordained priest in a parish adjacent to the university. After being shown into the priest's study, she took great care not to sound like a wild-eyed radical and explained as best she could how she had been studying recent developments in philosophy, the natural sciences, and cosmology. In an almost nonstop monologue she explained that she could understand how people could conceive of a God who is revealed in the natural and awesome processes of the universe. She talked about Catholic theologians Pierre Teilhard de Chardin and Thomas Berry and the interdisciplinary dialogue between scientists and theologians that she had been reading. "I believe," she said, "that God is with us through the simplest elements of nature, down to the smallest particles of atoms on the earth and in all of the universe." She ended almost breathless. The young priest looked at her with a blank stare and a slack jaw. It took him a full minute to re-spond. He then asked her how long it had been since she had been to confession. Angelle did not remember anything he said after that, except that he invited her to come back to the church.

Angelle never went back to church, but she continued to study and pray on her own. Duke died years later. She buried his chain in the park and placed a small cross of tree branches on top of it. In the years thereafter my wife and I every once in a while would walk with Angelle in the park with her new boxer, Gus. Angelle had discovered the sacredness of the universe but had no church community with whom to share it.

## Adult Spirituality

These stories are about spiritual awakenings. Through different events ultimate questions were raised, and the religious answers offered by churches were inadequate. In our case, my wife and I blamed our-selves for not developing an adult spirituality in our lives based upon the religious formation given to us as children. Bill's and Kathy's childhood experiences of religion also failed them, but the religion they found as adults almost led them to disaster. Laura's story has the same sense of failure with a mainline religious tradition that seemed out of touch with the contemporary questions of life and profession. Angelle's enthusiasm for her prayer life and desire to understand it met with a lack of understanding and little desire to listen to her experience.

For far too many adults religion has either lost its relevancy or has presented a regressive, dangerously naive view of life. The scan-dals of tele-evangelism, clergy pedophilia, and various other forms of abuse are all too obvious. These problems are the sensational ones that mass media love, maybe a little too much. And too many churches today treat their adult members as spiritual children. A childish spirituality is not appropriate for adults, and they know it. Yet, paradoxically, a childish spirituality keeps many adults tied to their churches. For most people, those ties retard adult growth through fear of death and an uncertain afterlife. It is true that the more com-plex life's problems are the more we seek simple answers. Religion can give simple, direct answers, but sometimes the answers are in-stead simplistic—the mark of childish spirituality.

Christian religion should be at the service of adult Christian spiri-tuality. Yet too often internal church political concerns take center stage and detract from the primary mission of church communities—

enabling adults to make religious sense of their lives. For this reason the majority of contemporary adults do not participate in church activities nor do they show any lasting allegiance. Most adults want to be thinking individuals and, at the same time, want to be part of some type of faith community.

We live in a fast-changing world. The anxiety of our era thrusts us toward questions of ultimacy at a time when world events and scientific discoveries occur at blinding speed. Our cultural "blindness" compels the need for direction, clarity, and vision—the stuff of spirituality. Adult Christian spirituality is an awakening to the search for meaning at the deepest levels of human experience. This awakening is not a singular event. It is a journey of discovery with periods of setback as well as advancement.

Most ministers are good-willed, highly motivated toward service to others, and want to do the right thing. Problems arise when they operate with outmoded models of spirituality, church structure, and Christian religious education. The hope for a vibrant future in most U.S. Christian denominations is to be found in matching the needs of people today with appropriate models of church and spiritual education. When this happens, the religious needs of people are met and the basic mission of Christianity becomes operative.

Church leaders have much to learn from the religiosity of We the People. Sociologists of religion and other researchers give valuable insights to the search for the sacred in a very uncertain world. While poll data can be somewhat hard to interpret, it can give important indications of the views that people hold. If theology and church life are to be at the service of spirituality, ministers need to be in touch with those views.

### CHRISTIANITY AS A CHURCH AT RISK

"I consider myself to be spiritual but not really religious." This commonly heard phrase characterizes the feelings that many Americans have about religion. According to a 1994 Gallup poll, only about a third (35%) of all Americans can be classified as religious. Yet almost all Americans say that they believe in God or a universal spirit (96%), and most of them (88%) say that religion is important in their lives.[2] Clearly, Americans yearn for spirituality, but they are not finding spiritual meaning in their religion. Typically, ministers characterize the American populace as spiritually lazy and describe U.S. culture as secular and godless. Many Americans, in turn, say that their churches and synagogues are out of touch with reality; they find little meaning in religious services. This clash of perceptions about religion and spirituality does not bode well for Christianity in the United States. In fact, Christianity is in crisis.

We have a crisis of opinion about the purpose of religion and the meaning of spirituality. Some ministers view spirituality as the sole province of religion. They see other expressions of spirituality as "flaky" religious experimentalism. Likewise, many Americans have written off formal Christian religion as incapable of providing meaningful spirituality. This conflict is complex because it involves deeply personal and often passionately held beliefs, as well as a lot of misconceptions about religion and spirituality.

Most adult Christians are simply not literate about their religion, and too many Christian ministers are not listening to the spiritual needs of church members, much less to the spiritual needs of U.S. popular culture. This crisis is not confined to one Christian denomination. It pervades all denominations, so much so that it places Christianity in the United States as a church at risk.

While it may seem problematic to refer to all Christian denominations as a single church, doing so makes two important points. First, Christianity has been pluriform from its beginnings. From their inceptions different Christian communities viewed their identity in somewhat disparate ways. St. Paul's epistles and the different perspectives that the gospel communities take on the life, death, and resurrection of Christ attest to diversity within early Christianity. Moreover, Christianity takes on different expressions and emphases in different cultures and in different time periods, not to mention the different interpretations of Christianity that occur within denominations. The chances of all Christian denominations coming together to form a single unified Christian church are about the same as the world having a single unified government. There are, however, a core set of beliefs in Jesus Christ as God and savior that link these very diverse denominations. The term *Christianity* recognizes the unity in the diversity of Christian denominations.

Second, Christian denominations face a common threat. Religious illiteracy places Christian adults at a distinct disadvantage in an important dimension of their lives. It also places U.S.Christianity at risk. The majority of Christians are silent as debate rages among liberals, conservatives, fundamentalists, and other groups struggling for power and influence. The majority are silent because they do not have a basis for evaluating who is right and who is wrong or even what the argument is really about. This situation promotes passivity, which eventually leads to disinterest and alienation. Unless

Christian denominations face the problem of adult religious illiteracy the relatively high weekly attendance rates in the United States (approximately 45%) will go the way of Europe, plummeting to approximately one-half that rate or lower. Christians rarely defect to other religions; rather, they disengage. Cultural Christians, those who identify themselves as Christians but do not attend services, are defecting in place but defecting nonetheless.[3]

Although this book focuses upon Christianity in the United States, the same need for understanding exists within all religions and among religions. The best way to accomplish this interreligious conversation is to know our own religion. It is often said that the more we know about our religion, the more secure we can be with the doubts that naturally come from belief in a mysterious God. This tentative comfort with uncertainty opens us to the plausibility of other religions. Yet, most adult Christians know very little about their religion. They depend upon their childhood Christian education and their religious practices as their base of knowledge about religion. But children and teens see and hear with the eyes, ears, and consciousness of their age. Misconceptions about religion can be born out of misunderstandings.

Knowing our religion also depends upon the quality of Christian education we receive in both childhood and adulthood. Too many ministers "water down" theology in Christian education classes and in their sermons. In some cases ministers do not have the knowledge to share. They are not informed about contemporary theological thought and depend upon the passion of their conviction to inspire their congregation. Some ministers profess that "faith in God is a simple matter; theology complicates faith unnecessarily." But nothing could be further from the truth. Good theology helps reasonable people understand their faith in deeper ways. The problem for some ministers is that mature faith informed by theology is threatening to them because mature faith is not receptive to control.

Spiritually educated people tend not to be passive. They question what some ministers do not want questioned. It is no wonder that adult conversation about religion either is avoided or soon lapses into a dispute. The majority of Christians in the United States are in dire need of religious education. The necessity for ecumenical dialogue between denominations is obvious, but there also exists a need for conversation between liberal and conservative movements within and among denominations.

The 1983 national education commission report *A Nation at Risk* mobilized communities locally and nationally to address the declining quality of public education.[4] Just as inadequate education places the United States as a nation at risk, adult spiritual illiteracy places Christianity in the United States as a church at risk. Adult spiritual illiteracy is not knowing how to address the ultimate questions of life and not knowing where to go to find answers. Where did we come from? Why are we here? Where are we going? These are only a few of many questions that have meaning at the deepest levels of human consciousness.

This spiritual illiteracy deepens the concept of a nation at risk. To be literate is to be empowered. To be illiterate, therefore, is to be disempowered. Spiritual literacy, in this age of increasing religious plurality both within and outside of Christianity, is an important aspect of what it means to be a literate person. As we enter the twenty-first century, spirituality is viewed as an increasingly important part of American public life. Thomas Jefferson and many others have long contended that a literate citizenry is crucial to the health of a democratic republic. Spiritual literacy, accordingly, is both a personal and a public necessity.

Knowing what we believe spiritually is often confused with knowing our religion. For example, Roman Catholics may have learned a great deal about the tenets of their religion by memorizing the catechism as children and adolescents. They may indeed have learned the catechism, but they may not have learned much about spirituality if their catechism answers did not help them address the ultimate concerns of everyday living. Likewise, Southern Baptists may have studied the Bible from childhood to adulthood through Sunday School classes. However, if they have not come to grips with what it means to be a thinking adult when interpretations of the Bible conflict with the prudent reason of a faithful person, they have not entered the realm of a mature spirituality. Each Christian denomination has the challenge of orienting itself toward the search for meaning at the deepest levels of human experience—levels so deep that we become aware of God.

An unconscious and unfortunate tendency of many ministers is to put the institutional concerns of religion above spirituality. Raising funds for church buildings, paying salaries, dealing with internal church conflicts, and the many other dimensions of institutional life can overwhelm the primary purpose of church life—mature spirituality. Most Americans consider these institutional preoccupations as reasons for religion's lack of relevancy. The common complaint, "My religion is getting in the way of my spirituality," expresses it well. Other adults fail to recognize the difference between these relatively minor institutional concerns and spirituality, and such in-house disputes take on a false sense of importance. Being able to recognize the difference is a matter of spiritual literacy.

The notion of a church at risk and a nation at risk might be heard from both the Religious Right and the Religious Left. Conservative and Evangelical religious movements call for religious literacy to preserve religious tradition as a way of life that "made this country great." Character and family values, they contend, are rooted in biblical understandings of right action in the world. Religious Right political movements have mobilized conservative and fundamentalist Christians over the past few decades to support or oppose political candidates on the basis of the candidates' moral and religious views. The Religious Right portrays the Religious Left as giving in to a secularized culture.

Religious Left movements, on the other hand, desire knowledge of religious tradition for very different reasons. Religious scholarship over the past century calls into question bedrock understandings of the Bible and religious tradition. The Religious Left movements in Christian churches of all denominations ask for investigation of religious tradition because of the increasing plurality and tolerance of opinion in contemporary life. Whether in New Age religious movements or liberal movements in mainline Christian denominations, biblical scholarship and religious tradition are examined in light of modern scholarship. Some radical Religious Left movements view Christian tradition as needing drastic revision, while more moderate movements try to influence current religious structures. Religious Left political movements are not as organized as the Religious Right. Liberal politics in general tends to be the platform for the Religious Left in reaction to the organizing efforts of the Religious Right. The Religious Left characterizes the Religious Right as intolerant religious totalitarians.

What are we to believe about these religious and political cultural wars? Most Americans have little or no basis for evaluating the adequacy of the Religious Right, Religious Left, or anything in between. Debates have the character of "sound bites." Terms like "gospel values," "Christian values" are thrown out as proofs of positions without any depth of meaning. Most Americans do not have the knowledge and background to be critical about what these code words really mean. The Christian religious education of most adults stopped somewhere between childhood and early adulthood.

There has been an outcry from many segments of U.S. culture denouncing the loss of the basic religious values that made this nation great. While there is a separation of church and state, there has not been a separation of religious values from the state. Common religious values undergird political, legal, and socioeconomic systems. U.S. currency proclaims "In God We Trust." We hold legal and political principles that support the dignity of the individual and inalienable human rights that ultimately have a religious base to them. The professions are struggling with ethics: business ethics, legal ethics, biomedical ethics, and so forth. The concept of virtue has recently gained prominence in the public arena.

All of these discussions have a religious and spiritual basis. Questions of morality and ethics in the public arena are viewed most often as somehow separated from religion. Yet they presume underlying assumptions about who or what God is, the right order of the universe, who human beings are, and the interrelationship of it all. In the urgency of the moment, we tend to focus on how to solve moral and ethical dilemmas without first addressing these basic assumptions. Put quite simply, most adults do not have an intelligent working framework for addressing religious questions.

This religious illiteracy is very dangerous because it sets up a false dualism between sacred and secular, a separation between religion and everyday life. Most adults have been taught that it is dangerous to think for themselves in religious matters. How many times have church members been given the "right" interpretation of scripture with absolute certainty by their ministers? How often have adult Christians been told, in subtle ways, that the role of church members is to "pray, pay, and obey"? Adult members are constantly given the message that they need the mediatory role of ministers to interpret the Bible, church tradition, and practices. To a great extent that mediatory role is correct. The problem is when mediation becomes control.

### Religious Literacy

The term *literacy* has a heavy sound to it; it carries a lot of power and connotes a lot of hard work. Learning to read and write is an all-important milestone for children. Without those skills, they have little access to education. Illiterate adults have very little power in U.S. culture. If one cannot read, it is almost impossible to succeed in life. Job possibilities tend to be limited to menial labor. An illiterate person is dependent upon literate family members and friends for many social interactions.

The literacy rate in the United States is over 95 percent, but there are many degrees of literacy. Those termed "functionally illiterate" can read and write, but not well enough to function in society. Their basic literacy skills cannot support their economic and social aspirations. In the United States, governmental and private foundations have mounted efforts to help illiterate adults learn to read and write. A primary factor in the success of such programs lies in the motivation of the adult learner. Few illiterate or functionally illiterate adults want to learn to read for the sheer pleasure of it. Rather, they want to read in order to get a job, win a promotion, or free themselves from feelings of social inadequacy.

Another way to view literacy is to focus on a particular area of life and culture. This notion of literacy presumes basic literacy skills and focuses upon gaining knowledge in a particular area. A person may want to be literate about U.S. history, or cancer research, or baseball, for instance. But the individual remains unknowledgeable (illiterate) about it because he or she does not have the motivation or the expertise to gain that knowledge. Education provides the process and the resources for those who desire to be literate.

Very often there are misconceptions about the need for religious literacy. For many people, knowledge of religion means knowledge of religious practices and a sense of piety. The problem is that such knowledge tends not to be empowering. It is imitative. It can restrict the meaning of religion to familiar practices and the interpretation of religious experts (ministers). There are also problems with a solely intellectual approach to religious literacy. One cannot be truly literate about a religion without participating in it. In other words, simply reading about or studying a religion does not impart the fullness of its meaning.

Religious literacy, therefore, depends upon a foundational principal—motivation—with two secondary elements—education and participation. For adults, motivation comes from the meaning that they receive from religion. Even though it sounds somewhat irreligious, religious meaning is intimately connected with usefulness. Adults have very little patience with religious practices that do not meet their spiritual needs. In other words, religion should be at the service of spirituality. This does not mean that religion simply should be a "feel good" affair catering to the fashionable whims of the moment. Religion should constantly invite adults to look for deeper meaning in life. Sometimes that meaning comes in the form of a challenge, a call to action. Other times it is encouragement and nourishment to deal with a seemingly hostile world. In any case, churches need to motivate their members to search for deeper meaning in life, and members need to hold church leaders accountable to their primary purpose for being—the promotion of spirituality. Put in Christian terms, Christ did not come to save himself. He was a person for others. Christian churches, therefore, do not exist for the purpose of their own survival; they exist for people. When Christian churches embrace spirituality as their foundational motivation for existence, education and participation naturally follow. Education then becomes spiritual education, and participation in the life of the church community becomes attractive.

Spiritual education promotes religious literacy. Churches that embrace spiritual education offer many ways that assist their members to find meaning in an often confusing world. Educational programs are as varied as their members. Traditional courses and workshops on scripture and church tradition are offered in convenient formats and promote a sense of community. A hallmark of these educational programs is their sense of educational process. Most adults have had unsatisfying educational experiences. This "educational baggage" is carried into each adult educational setting and needs to be overcome.

A particular world view pervades current models of Christian church life and places Christianity at risk in the United States. For lack of better terminology, we name this world view *fundamentalistic*. The contention is that fundamentalism, despite its popularity, does not promote mature spirituality. Christian churches need to find their way into a new paradigm for being church in order to be relevant and to prepare for the future. A key to making church relevant is found in a world view that fulfills basic religious needs that fundamentalism wrongly satisfies. I term this world view *Christian spiritual humanism*. Assistance in the formation of a mature adult spirituality that makes sense for people today is the goal of Christian spiritual humanism. A major aspect of this different world view is a model of education in which churches educate adults about the richness of Christian tradition, and adults educate churches about their experience in the world. We might then speak of spiritual education instead of the Christian religious education of the past. This emerging type of education presumes that Christianity is meant to make a difference in the lives of people and the earth that we share.

The Christian influence on religiosity in the United States is overwhelming. Some surprises, however, are to be found in poll data on religiosity over the past fifty years and from sociological analysis as well. A closer look at different models of faith and motivations for connection with church communities can yield insights into how churches can best meet the spiritual needs of their members and others in the popular culture. Typically, U.S. Christian churches have operated with the intention of forming their members according to the ministers' understanding of the Bible and religious practices. But ordinary church members and even non-church members have religious experience as well. Churches need to listen to the spiritual awakenings that are occurring in our time.

# RELIGIOSITY
# IN AMERICAN LIFE

✝

The stories we related in chapter 1 are specific instances of what occurs on a large scale in the American religious landscape. Locating our individual stories within a larger framework can be helpful. It is comforting to know that we are not alone in our struggle with religious questions and that our need for spirituality is part of the human condition.

A primary way to bring spirituality to expression is through religion. The problem is that too many Christian churches have lost sight of this basic reason for existence. This chapter presents four ways of viewing religion in the United States: sociological models of religiosity trends, models of church affiliation, stages of faith, and an examination of religious relevancy. In each framework we see psychosocial trends and human developmental stages that are typical in U.S. Christianity. The sociological models give us a large-scale look at religious trends over the past fifty years. Models of church affiliation can help us to understand periods in our lives in which we feel a strong connection to church and periods in which we pull away from church communities. The stages-of-faith framework provides a developmental guide to faith and spirituality at a deeply personal level. These stages have a profound effect on church and society. Finally, religious relevancy is examined from the perspective of three interrelated inconsistencies found in U.S. religiosity. The chapter ends with the concept of vocation as a way of addressing problems raised by this psychosocial analysis.

## Models of U.S. Religiosity

Sociologists have differing views about religion and American religious attitudes. Most often the assumption is that Americans are not as religious as they were in the past. But U.S. survey data and sociological research since the 1940s present a more complicated scenario, as well as some surprises about popular attitudes toward religion. There are five models of how and why religiosity in the United States has changed over the past fifty years.[1] As with most models, there is some truth to be found in all of them.

### Secularization

The secularization model assumes that the more educationally sophisticated and technological U.S. society becomes, the more people will choose reason and science rather than traditional religion as ways of making sense out of life. The assumption is that most religious traditions are inconsistent and out of step with contemporary life. According to this model, religion will become less and less important in American life.

Sociologist Andrew Greeley contends that the secularization model fits only U.S. attitudes about sexual ethics and belief in a literal interpretation of the Bible.[2] Surveys indicate an increase in premarital sex and divorce rates since the early 1960s. It remains unclear, however, whether or not this shift in sexual behavior is due to secularization of society or to increased availability and technology of birth-control methods. Likewise, more effective birth-control methods coupled with greater demand and acceptance of women in the work place could account for these changes in sexual ethics as well.[3]

Survey data also indicate a decline in the percentage of people who believe in a literal interpretation of the Bible, that is, that every word in the Bible should be taken as the actual word of God. In the early 1960s approximate 65 percent of those surveyed believed in literal interpretation of the Bible. By the late 1960s the percentage deceased to less than 40 percent, and the figure is now just above 30 percent. Greater availability of higher education seems to be a factor in this decreased acceptance of a literal interpretation of the Bible. In 1991, 58 percent of survey respondents who believed in literal interpretation of the Bible had not graduated from high school, while only 14 percent were college graduates.[4]

### Cyclical Variations

The cyclical model holds that U.S. attitudes about religion have alternately intensified and weakened over the past fifty years. It is to be expected that the religious pendulum will swing from periods of cynicism to religious fervor partly because of current events. Just as there are swings in the popularity of liberalism and conservatism, so are there swings in the popularity of religiosity and secularization.

Some pollsters suggest that long-term trends indicate a cyclical pattern in the influence of religion on society.[5] In 1957, a time of relative social stability, 69 percent of Americans believed that religion's influence on American life was increasing. In 1970, when social institutions were in disarray, only 14 percent of Americans believed that religion's influence on American life was increasing. Yet, in 1985, that percentage went back up to 49 percent. Thus, there seems to be a cyclical pattern of perceptions about whether the influence of religion in American life is increasing or decreasing. The meaning of this indicator, however, may have more to do with general perceptions about society than about religion. In other words, opinions about the relevance of religion may stay the same, but perceptions about society's acceptance of religion may vary.[6]

### Episodic Events

The episodic shock model focuses upon unusual events that affect religion in the United States. A striking Roman Catholic example is the effects that the Second Vatican Council (1962–65) had upon Catholic religious life in the late 1960s and the following decades. The council documents made sweeping changes that led some Catholics to a new sense of religious freedom, yet it left many more with a great deal of uncertainty. The tele-evangelist scandals of the Bakkers, Jimmy Swaggart, and others in the 1980s are other examples of episodic shock. These scandals brought down vast television empires and left many Christians believing that religion is filled with hypocrisy.

The episodic shock model seems to apply primarily to church attendance rates. Some event or series of events will cause a decline in attendance for a period of time. In Roman Catholicism, for example, the weekly church attendance rate fell sharply from 1969 to 1975. Greeley attributes that decline to the dissemination of *Humanae Vitae*, the papal encyclical that banned artificial means of birth control for Catholics. He contends that this highly contested church teaching undermined U.S. Catholics' loyalty to their church. That particular episodic shock apparently has waned in the 1990s. In 1991, the

Catholic weekly attendance rate of 51 percent was slightly higher than the Protestant rate of 45 percent.[7] The same thing might be said of the tele-evangelist scandals. Jimmy Swaggart and at least one of the Bakkers returned to television after their fall from grace in attempts to rebuild their ministries.

## Religious Growth

The religious growth model is the most optimistic about religion's growth in society. It assumes that there is an innate tendency in human beings and their society to grow ever more religious as time passes. This model presumes that churches are meeting the religious needs of society and that religious hunger increases as society develops. This growth could also come from an increasing ability of religions to meet the religious needs of society.

There is little evidence to support the religious growth model. Even though Bible reading has increased over the past century and other measures of religiosity have increased as well, there also is evidence that many measures of religiosity have decreased. The Princeton Religion Research Center Index is a composite of many indicators of U.S. religiosity: belief in God, religious denominational preference, perceptions about the relevance of religion, confidence in church and clergy, and so forth. The index reached a high of 746 (out of a possible 1000 points) in 1956. It took its steepest decline in the decade of the 1980s, a 30–point dip from 681 in 1980 to 651 in 1990.[8] In the 1980s the tele-evangelist scandals as well as deepened conflicts between clergy over church issues resulted in some sharp divisions between clergy and laity. Many issues surfaced, such as abortion rights, the question of women's ordination, and crystallization of conservative and liberal camps in many Christian denominations.

## Stability

The stability model maintains that basic religious beliefs and practices remain the same over time. The reason is that religiosity is a human instinct and that religious change amounts to little more than variations on ancient themes. Thus, change over the period of a few decades or even a century is minimal.

Greeley, somewhat surprisingly, contends that the stability model of religiosity best fits the American situation,[9] though he is at odds with many sociologists who believe that secularization is more descriptive of American life. Greeley argues that there is comparatively little difference in American basic religious beliefs over the past half-century: belief in God, the divinity of Jesus, life after death, the existence of heaven, and divine influence on the Bible. There are some changes in how the Bible is interpreted (either the literal word or inspired word of God) and other nuances, but the basic beliefs, he maintains, remain much the same.

My inclination is to agree generally with Greeley's analysis. This basic set of Christian beliefs is supported by current parlance about family values, character, virtue, and American culture in general. For better or worse, these religious values are what most Americans mean by the "religious values that made this nation great." The problem is with the *interpretation* of this set of beliefs. While the great majority of Americans (84 percent) believe in God as a heavenly father who can be reached by prayers, what that belief means in a person's life can vary greatly.[10] For some people, it gives to a mysterious God a familiar human role so that they can more readily identify with God. For others, it literally means a heavenly father somewhere in the universe who looks over human affairs. Likewise, for some adults, prayer means divine intervention into life; for others, it means the granting of strength to endure life's hardships. Poll data and interviews with Americans on their religious beliefs can be hard to interpret. Nonetheless, I believe that Greeley is more right than wrong about relatively little change in basic religious beliefs over the past half-century. There is much more to this story, however.

### STAGES OF RELIGIOUS AFFILIATION

Robert Bezilla utilizes data gathered from The Princeton Religion Research Center polls over the past fifty years to describe nine stages of religious affiliation that typical U.S. residents have throughout their lives.[11] These stages describe how people tend to relate to churches. Each of the stages gives an insight into how church life can fulfill basic human and social needs. The stages also give hints about how closely spirituality is tied to the present concerns of everyday living.

### *Stage One—Early Childhood*

Stage one is best characterized by the desires of parents (see stage six). Most Christian parents want their children to receive some type of religious education and find it important to take them to church, Sunday School, or religious instruction of various types. Because of this desire to pass on religious values to their children, parents tend to be very active in church activities themselves during this stage.

### Stage Two—Early Teens

Early teens are most likely to mirror the religious attitudes of their parents and their church. Youth-group events and similar gatherings are important because of the need for group identification and belonging. Organized church activities provide a way to negotiate the awkwardness of this stage of life.

### Stage Three—Older Teens

The period starting with age sixteen or so is a time in which teens try to decide for themselves whether or not they will go to church. Wider social groupings and dating often compete with church functions and allegiance for time and interests. This broader social life may also include first exposures to other denominations and faiths.

### Stage Four—Higher Education

This is a time of investigating and challenging the assumptions of childhood and teenage years and of encountering many different conceptions of religion. This stage also marks either a formal or an informal introduction to different philosophies of life. Many college students become much less active in their church life, but few lose their basic faith. Young people who take jobs or enter the armed services also experience introductions to different mentors and, in turn, have their religious assumptions challenged.

### Stage Five—Young Adulthood

Young adulthood is a period of challenge to religious formation, and many young adults lose their interest in religion. Over the past fifty years this stage has tended to move from a period in the early twenties to thirty-something. Young adults in this stage tend to be without children and are experimenting with religious meaning in their lives.

### Stage Six—Family Formation

This stage begins when adults start having children. The trend here also seems to be moving toward the thirty-year-old age group from the early twenty-year-old group of the past. If these adults have left their church, this is the time that they are inclined to return. They want to contribute to the building of their church community and want their children to receive religious education.

### Stage Seven—Middle Age

The middle years mark a spiritual turning point for many people. These years may be the most active period of church affiliation, with involvement in different types of lay ministry. Or this stage may be characterized by an alienation from church. Divorce, separation, estrangement from children, or some type of midlife crisis may drive individuals away from church. Since children are grown or almost grown, church affiliation now must meet personal meaning needs.

### Stage Eight—Grandparenting

Grandparenting can provoke renewed interest in church. As in the family formation stage, the primary motivation for grandparents is the religious education of their grandchildren. They want their grandchildren to receive religious formation in their church.

### Stage Nine—Old Age

Old age has less to do with deathbed conversions than a change in the church needs of individuals. By this stage in life, religious beliefs tend to be firmly set. Being widowed or separated from family makes it more difficult to be an active member of a church community, but those who find ways to remain active receive comfort from their church community. Churches should be aware of the communal needs of seniors.

Through Bezilla's analysis we see the typical phases of religious belonging and the motivations behind them. Stated differently, We the People find meaning in belonging to a church, but that belonging tends to be on our own terms. Just as in voluntary organizations, belonging to a church moves from membership out of a sense of duty, propriety, or even social standing to membership out of a sense of personal need.

A particular type of U.S. religiosity, therefore, is alive and well. Core values about religious belief have been relatively stable over the past fifty years, yet church attendance rates have fallen and the importance of religion in everyday life has decreased as well. Are Christian churches at fault? Perhaps churches are at risk if ministers are unaware of or ignore the needs of people at different stages of life.

### FAITH DEVELOPMENT

Stages of religious affiliation give us a sense of why people belong to a church. But not everyone belongs or participates actively. Another way of approaching the question of religiosity is through an investigation of faith. In an effort to understand how faith affects our lives, James Fowler describes in *Stages of Faith* a series of developmental stages that most people tend to negotiate at different times in life.[12] Fowler describes our quest to make sense out of our lives as an innate human desire for religiosity and a natural process of development. His introduction to the text sounds like the personal awakening stories with which we started. He paints a picture of waking up in the middle of the night in a cold sweat of fear and doubt. In that moment he was a stranger to himself. All of the faith constructions that gave contour and structure to his life were stripped away by deep anxiety. Without his faith, he was disoriented. As Fowler puts it, "Faith helps us form a dependable 'life space,' an ultimate environment. At a deeper level, faith undergirds us when our life space is punctured and collapses, when the felt reality of our ultimate environment proves to be less than ultimate."[13] For Fowler, faith is fundamental to the human constitution. Faith develops no less than our intellect and the other ways we grow as human beings. Thus, to be human is to be a person of faith. Obviously, Fowler is not describing the faith of a particular religion, although his research is primarily in Christian contexts.

Fowler makes important distinctions among faith, religion, and belief.[14] He describes *religion* as a "cumulative tradition" made up of scripture, rituals, symbols, law, creeds, prophecies, myths, ethical teachings, community, and the many other characteristics of religious practice. Religion is cumulative because of its ongoing development. It utilizes past elements to create new ones in order to address the contemporary situation. Religion, however, serves a deeper purpose. It should be at the service of faith.

*Faith* is deeper and more personal than religion. It is the human quest for relationship to transcendence. And transcendence describes the many ways in which we reach out beyond ourselves to connect with the ultimate questions of life—those mysterious, seemingly unanswerable questions that gnaw at us: Who is God? What is my relationship to God and to other people? Why does a loving God allow evil and suffering in this world? In the realm of ultimacy, I become mysterious to myself. Who am I? Where did I come from? Why am I here? Where am I going? What happens when I die? What is my relationship to the rest of the earth and the universe? Faith is a basic orientation to the world; it shapes our world view.

*Belief*, on the other hand, has come to mean something much different now than it did in the past. Prior to the sixteenth century, *to believe* meant to "set one's heart, to hold dear, to love." It basically meant to affirm one's faith, to be dedicated to a community of faith. As Western culture developed, *belief* lost that meaning. Belief today has less to do with one's world view and more to do with giving assent to a proposition or set of propositions. In our era we tend to ask what the beliefs of a particular religion are. It is like saying that we can capsulate a religious tradition into a set of propositions. Fowler contends that for premodern societies *belief* and *faith* are verbs rather than nouns. For them, "faithing" is like that premodern sense of believing. *Faith(ing)*, as a verb, connotes active engagement. *Faith*, as a noun, sounds like content, a deposit of faithing activity.

Fowler's distinctions are important. Our current fascination with trying to understand the beliefs (facts) about our religion or those of other religions will never capture the heart of what it means to belong to that religion. The only way to understand what it really means to be Baptist, Catholic, Lutheran, or a member of any other church is to be part of those communities with all of their unspoken values, rituals, ways of gathering, and implicit attitudes toward God and the world. Likewise, the only way to understand a particular religion is to understand how and why its members "set their hearts." In this sense, we recognize that religion at its finest is helping shape a particular world view, a way of being in the world. It is at the service of faith. This makes religion a wonderful way to give meaning to our lives.

At the same time, and for the same reasons, religion can be very dangerous. For Bill and Kathy, in chapter 1, the religious world view they received from the preacher at a large local motel almost killed Kathy and their baby. Fortunately, my wife and I discovered a religious world view that gave us new life. The difference is not necessarily that the content—the facts—of our religion are better than other religious traditions. Rather, we were fortunate enough to have our religion presented to us in a way that helped give contour to a religious world view that made sense to us. It led us to growth. The mark of effective religion is that it can provide a religious world view that leads to growth toward spiritual maturity. If it cannot, then it is something less—and very dangerous.

In Fowler's framework faith is imaginative, a way of landscaping our world. Beliefs point to a mysterious world that we try to landscape. Religion, therefore, with all of its beliefs and cumulative traditions, gives shape to faith, not the other way around. Religion should be a barometer of the health of faith, constantly checking whether it is promoting growth in faith. Faith is a human universal; everyone has it. It is religion's task to make it evident, concrete, and to give it depth.

Fowler has identified seven stages of faith. More empirical work needs to be done to test his stages in other religious contexts. Feminist theologians and developmental researchers critique Fowler's work because they claim it is based upon a masculine framework of separation, individuation, and achievement. Researchers suggest that men and women may use the same vocabulary about moral and faith development, but their language means very different things. It could be that women are much more focused upon relationship rather than achievement in moral and faith life.[15] In any case, there is enough resemblance for us in Fowler's work to warrant a quick look.

Before outlining different stages of faith, it would be good to discuss the structure of faith development. Stages of faith could be viewed as climbing a ladder or a set of stairs to be an ever more faithful person. Fowler (like other developmentalists) correlates the stages with chronological stages of human development. Thus, it seems logical that stage six is "better than" stage five, but that is not what Fowler intends. Stages of faith do not refer to the content or quality of faith but to the structure of faith. Describing the structure of faith is like portraying how we go about describing our world view. Our view of life seems unlimited until we see that there is something beyond the horizon. When something beyond the horizon becomes visible, we know that the world is larger than we imagined. Moving from one stage of faith to another is like moving from one horizon to the next, making our world a bit more complex with each move.

The horizon metaphor describes Fowler's idea about our faith life better than the ladder or set of stairs image. In each stage our world view represents the way we tend to view life. Stage six is more complex than stage five because the complexity of how we view faith and the many ways we make sense out of life is more complex. Having a particular world view does presume certain ways of knowing, believing, and valuing. When those ways of making sense out of the world change, then we are compelled to change. And that is not always a pleasant process. It does not mean we in stage six are better persons than those in stage five. Rather, stage six is a representation of a particular world view. Faithfulness and nobility are to be found in each world view. The following brief snapshots give only hints of what Fowler describes more fully as stages of faith.[16]

### Stage One—Primal Faith

As infants we come screaming into this world with a lot of needs. In coming to a sense of what it means to be an individual, the infant forms primal images of good and bad, trust and mistrust, vulnerability and comfort. The first symbols of faith are maternal and paternal presence. Their reliability shape our images of superordinary power that have a lot to do with our later images of God. The child wonders if parents can be trusted to return once out of sight. These images and feelings are inarticulate but powerful.

I can remember my daughter, as an infant, reaching out and clinging to my wife and me for complete support. How powerful those memories must be for a child. They are powerful for my wife and me as well. At times when I was holding my daughter I would look at those bright blue eyes staring at me and wonder what she was thinking or feeling. Imagine what it means for a child not to have that support or for that support to be inconsistent. Most certainly those very early years of security or insecurity affect a person's world view and the way he or she perceives God in later life. My wife and I were the center of our daughter's faith, and to a great extent her presence, her life, embodied the heart of our faith.

### Stage Two—Intuitive-Projective Faith

Our world becomes more complex as we begin to use language (age two or so). We learn to construct and interact with our world in new ways. At this age we create imaginative, intuitive fantasy constructs and project them to make our world. Logical operations that sort out these feelings will come later. As children we form powerful perceptions about God. Vivid imagery of Bible stories and many other stories of faith are very important; the narrative is secondary to the texture of the imagery.

In this stage there is a fluid nature to our meaning-making, and the ability to take on the perspective of others is typically not developed. The baby Jesus, the manger, and the three kings are far more important at this age than details about the story. The way things look, sound, and feel trigger imagination about who God is and about our relationship with God. Our world is supple, fantasy-filled, and intuitively constructed from our egocentrism. At this stage we "soak up" images of God, death, life, hope, disappointment, and other realities from images presented in the popular culture. Images of God, therefore, can have their origin in an amalgam of parental figures, Bible stories, religious pictures and stories, television and movie heroes, and an occasional purple dinosaur. A rich imagination is the gift of this stage. But, conversely, dramatic, powerful imagery can unwittingly anchor future conceptions of God, church, and morality in ways that may become rather rigid.

It was shocking to me that my daughter, at this age, viewed God as a person in the sky who looked down upon us to see if we were doing the right thing. My wife and I tried to convey an image of God as loving creator. Yet this other image was perhaps more influential. Where did it come from? It could be that the image came from the expectations that we had for our daughter; namely, to do the right thing. I suspect that a more complete answer is to be found in a mix of church services, some Bible stories, her friends, her preschool teachers, and many images of God that came to her through the popular culture. In this stage of faith my daughter was not bothered by conflicting images. This fluid imagery of God (loving creator versus judge) was projected back to her world to suit her needs.

The transition from the intuitive-projective stage to the next stage of complexity in world view occurs with the onset of concrete operational thinking. The imaginative world of the preschooler is a mixture of fantasy, fact, and feeling. Concrete operational thinking includes the ability to construct a more orderly, dependable world. Both inductive and deductive reasoning develops. This transition makes possible the more complex world view of mythic-literal faith.

### Stage Three—Mythic-Literal Faith

As we enter school age, the mythic narrative structure of stories becomes more important. While imagination and feelings are still very important, being able to tell or retell a story accurately (literally) and perhaps with added richness takes on more relevance. Concepts of right and wrong, fairness, and reward and punishment become more developed. Faith, in this stage, is more a matter of knowing the stories, values, and rules of our family and tradition in order to make sense out of an increasingly complex world.

In the previous stage, we heard and felt the stories of others; self-created stories had little narrative logic to them. In this stage we are able to create stories—our own stories. Fantasy and imagination are still very important, but the ability to create narratives—myth, drama, story—comes from being able to take on the perspective of others along with an improved grasp of cause-and-effect relationships. This increased ability and interest in narrative creates an interest in stories of faith as well as in the beliefs and practices of our religion.

The fluid nature of meaning in the previous stage gives way to a desire to know, literally, what is true or untrue, right or wrong. Meanings behind stories, however, are not readily accessible to us in this stage. Story becomes a primary way to achieve this certainty and add coherence to a world view. Just as story gives coherence to world view, the principle of reciprocity—mutual fairness—becomes a primary moral motivation. Justice, in this stage, means doing unto others as they do unto you.

The strength of this stage is appreciation for the potency of story and narrative expression. It orders a world view with concreteness and power. Literalism, however, can create a world view in which religion is viewed as primarily controlling meaning through the actions of its heroes as portrayed in religious stories, myths, and practices. As Fowler puts it, "For this stage the meaning is both carried and 'trapped' in the narrative."[17] This literalism also is expressed in a one-dimensional understanding of symbol. The idea that symbols can have many layers of meaning is uncomfortable for us in this world view.

The Santa Claus myth was a hot topic for my daughter and her friends in her first year or so of elementary school. At one point she quite proudly announced to my wife and me that she did not believe in Santa Claus. When we explained the meaning behind the story of Santa Claus, she knowingly nodded her head, but that meaning carried little weight compared to her certainty that the story itself was not true. In her eyes she had grown up. We can readily see the limitations of a child's world view in this stage of faith.

My maternal grandfather spent his life in one of the immigrant ghettos of New Orleans. I can only remember him as being retired from work and old. He was a very good man who raised twelve children with my grandmother. She died quite a few years before him; he died at the age of ninety. The statues and blessed candles that he kept in his bedroom were curiosities for me. It appeared that his spirituality revolved around those symbols of faith—the saints, the holy water, and the many religious rituals and celebrations of the year. There seemed to be a beautiful simplicity to his faith. Duty was first and foremost in his religious life, and that duty was mediated through faith symbols that had very concrete meanings for him.

I did not know him well enough to characterize his faith world view as being mythic-literal. But I can understand how emphasis on a literal interpretation of religious symbols formed an important part of his faith. Despite the significant changes in Catholicism during his life, including some of the church saints being understood as legendary figures instead of actual people, his statuary was not altered. Changing those symbols would have, no doubt, been a crisis.

### Stage Four—Synthetic-Conventional Faith

Around early adolescence the conflict of different versions of stories, beliefs, and values becomes problematic for perhaps the first time. How can God be a person and be everywhere at the same time? How can God love people and allow bad things to happen to them? The need for some sort of synthesis arises. A settling, or integration, of beliefs and values becomes not only possible because of increased intellectual capabilities, it becomes a necessity. This synthesis is a way of creating our identity as faith-filled persons. It is a personal struggle, yet we draw upon resources found in religious concepts and authority figures who represent the conventional wisdom of our religion.

Many of us settle into this stage of faith during our adolescence and continue in it for the rest of our life. This stage of faith seems to be promoted by most religious traditions. Religion typically tries to answer religious questions and promote religious identity. In this stage we continually try to synthesize the many aspects of our faith world in light of the conventional wisdom of our religious tradition. Another way of phrasing it is that we look to our religious tradition to help us make sense out of life. We assume that our religious leaders can assist us with the continual challenge of synthesizing and constructing our landscape of faith.

The concern with identity in this stage overshadows the need for objective answers to complicated questions of faith. The tacit assumptions of faith are enough for stability in this stage. The symbols of faith and friendships are primary ways in which meaning is expressed. Emotional support carried through symbols and friendships is a powerful way of making sense out of life amid its vagaries. A rigorous examination of the propositions of faith, understandably, is not a felt need.

The synthetic-conventional stage can accommodate a generalized sense of faith in the popular culture. Very often this faith cannot be articulated because it has not been questioned in depth. This type of faith underlies what often is called cultural or civil religion.[18] For people without close ties to a church, the search for stability in their faith life centers around social institutions or movements that they trust. Faith in one's country is an expression of a powerful meaning structure for some people. The U.S. flag and other national symbols are significant marks of virtue, honor, duty, and righteousness for some people. Coupled with the community aspects of participation in veterans' organizations and other public-spirited groups, patriotism can constitute a powerful faith system. Different types of cultural movements also can provide faith structures. The Civil Rights movement has had many symbolic expressions of faith, community, and relationships that constitute a significant faith commitment for many people. For some, it is their primary faith community. For others, animal rights or environmental groups provide similar faith structure.

This stage of faith can be very comfortable for church ministers. There tends to be little questioning of religious authority and a high tolerance for inconsistency in doctrine and in practice. This stage can be the religious equivalent of an "America, love it or leave it" attitude. Religious structures are taken for granted. Alternative structures are not considered because people in this stage of faith have given assent to an "ideology" that supports the status quo. But the ideology is not tightly organized. People tend to be "at home" in this stage of faith. It can provide a powerful meaning-making structure. Adults can interpret a more or less consistent cluster of values and beliefs in ways they find useful. There is room for varieties of opinion so long as they are not completely out of range of common denominators. People in this stage of faith find it easy to criticize individuals because of mistakes or lack of faith but would not think of criticizing the structure of their religion or faith system.

A dark side of this stage is the indictment, often a self-indictment, of those who do not fit in with the status quo. A lot of guilt accumulates in a person who has not lived according to the conventions of a particular religion. A Catholic friend told me of an uncle who moved from town after marrying a previously divorced Catholic woman. He had not attended weddings of relatives back in his hometown for thirty years because of his illicit marriage. He did not attend because the ceremonies included Mass, and he could not receive communion. He did not go to confession because he felt that he had done nothing wrong. Nonetheless, he was consumed with guilt and alienation.

### Stage Five—Individuative-Reflective Faith

In late adolescence and early adulthood there often is a transition from the synthetic-conventional stage of faith to this next stage. As in previous stages, many of us may stay in this stage the rest of our lives. Also, many adults who enter this stage may not do so until they reach their mid-thirties or forties.

The transition to the individuative-reflective stage involves two essential features: a critical distancing from our previous assumptive value system, and the emergence of authority within the self.[19] Often there is a physical move involved—to college or the world of work, to marriage, or to one or more of the many other ways in which young adults move out on their own. When we move from one location to another, it sometimes is easier to view the world in which we lived with all of its assumptions about propriety and impropriety, right and wrong, good and bad. We tend to look critically at what we left behind.

The emergence of authority within the self, the executive ego, often accompanies such a move, but not always. Being on one's own involves making critical choices. Some choose to reject the church of their childhood. Others reject their family values or traditional American values. The college experience, for example, is often a lightning rod for critical inquiry and rejection of childhood faith constructs.

In some cases the authorities of childhood faith that have been left behind are simply replaced by other authority figures: college professors, military service officers, corporate officials, in-laws, and so forth. Thus, one faith system is replaced by another without critical reflection on the faith itself.

The move to an individuative-reflective faith stage involves negotiating both transition features. Along with critically examining our assumptive world, we take authority for our own meaning-making. This stage is "individuative" in that it involves taking personal responsibility for holding a particular world view. We find meaning less from significant others and conventional roles and more from an awareness of a world view to which we freely give assent. This stage is "reflective" because of our willingness to reflect critically upon social systems and institutions that give structure to faith. We also place symbols, doctrines, and practices under critical scrutiny—a demythologizing approach to faith.

The difficulty with this stage is that the demythologizing may be somewhat crude or incomplete. Some may assume an either/or mentality—"Either it's true or it's not true." In a search for historical accuracy the meaning behind Bible stories or traditional myths may be lost. Moreover, there could be an inadequate appreciation for the power and intensity of symbols. These instincts are often found in people engaging in scripture or theological scholarship for the first time. Very often a student's assumptive world is challenged by the scholarship. The process of deconstruction begins with no sense of reconstruction in sight.

### Stage Six—Conjunctive Faith

Crucial to entering this stage is an experience of the "sacrament of defeat" and the reality of living out faith commitments.[20] The "sacrament of defeat" occurs when a deep loss or disappointment shatters the certainty of the executive ego and world view that was built in the previous stage. A person typically does not enter this stage before midlife.

The meaning of the "sacrament of defeat" is evident in the following story. John was a partner in a newly formed small manufacturing company. Becoming a partner in the company was the dream of a lifetime. Previously he had worked in sales and sales management for large corporations and had found that either he was not rewarded for his work or he was taken advantage of by upper management. Now he was to *be* upper management, and things would be different.

The newly formed company had three partners. John was in charge of sales, and things got off to a fast start. But the company soon ran into problems with production. The company produced precision parts, but the machinists were not up to the task of manufacturing parts fast enough. Deliveries were delayed, and therefore revenue was not coming in. The company had a large business loan to pay off, so the senior partner decided that each partner would invest a substantial amount of money to keep the company afloat for the next thirty days. John disagreed. He contended that the problem could be taken care of with better production. An argument ensued, and the senior partner fired John. His dream was shattered.

Although John's previous employer called to offer him his job back, John's despair was so deep that he could not even talk about it. He had placed his trust in hard work and determination, but disappointment resulted instead of success. He had encountered setbacks in the past, but this time it was different. John said that the American dream was a lie, that for the first time he could understand why people commit suicide.

John had recently reconciled with his religion. Through Sunday School classes and a Bible study group, John had become acquainted with historical biblical scholarship and church history. Religion was making sense to him for the first time. John had actually prayed about his business decision. And his choice resulted in the biggest disappointment of his life. But defeat became a sacrament when John's wife calmly said to him, "Let's do something more meaningful with our lives." John looked at his wife and two-year-old daughter and replied, "Yes, it's time."

This defeat could have led John to suicide or a very cynical, despairing outlook toward life. For John, it symbolized a crashing in of his world view—of the American dream and his religion. John had a choice of constructing and embracing the next stage of faith or staying in the same stage and trying to sort out what happened to him while clinging to the same world view. Both John and his wife became educators. They now talk about the American dream to young people in ways that they would not have previously imagined.

A person in the conjunctive faith stage appreciates the power of symbol and the need to live with paradox in one's life. Symbols take on layered, multiple meanings beyond logical reasoning. Objective critique is turned onto itself by questioning the assumptions that are the foundations for objective reality.

Conjunctive faith joins disparate points of view in the search for truth. We seek comprehensive and inclusive frameworks for justice and moral decision-making. We become more comfortable living in the "gray areas" of life than we were in the past. Life takes on greater thickness and complexity. We see the truth-claims of faith as partial expressions of greater truth. Clear-cut categories of right and wrong, good and bad, become more problematic. In this stage we can neither view these problems as we did in the past nor ignore them. Rather, we are compelled to struggle with the problems.

### *Stage Seven—Universalizing Faith*

This last stage in Fowler's schema represents mature faith. He describes it in the most inclusive terms he can, while at the same time acknowledging the Jewish-Christian framework with which he is most familiar. Adults in this stage create "zones of liberation" from oppressive social structures, are oriented toward a universal conception of community, love life but "hold it loosely," and are open to people in other stages of faith and from other faith traditions.[21] Fowler cites such famous examples as Gandhi; Martin Luther King, Jr.; Mother Teresa of Calcutta; Dietrich Bonhoeffer; Abraham Heschel; and Thomas Merton.

Fame need not be the mark of universalizing faith, however. But a willingness to stand up for recognizing truth and God beyond the confines of conventional wisdom is a mark of this stage. People in this stage of faith act upon their convictions. They determine the morally right thing to do with the most inclusive interests in mind and actually do it. They may be persecuted or put to death for going against the grain of society; their faithfulness may not be recognized until after their death.

Universalizers do not have their heads in the sky; they see the redemptive possibilities in the concrete situations in which they find themselves. Ordinary events call forth the power to act upon their faith in extraordinary ways. The result of their actions need not have profound effects in the larger culture. But their actions can have profound effects on individuals, families, churches, and local communities. We are fortunate, indeed, if we have encountered (and recognized) a universalizer in our lives.

RELIGIOUS RELEVANCY

George Gallup, Jr., and Jim Castelli point out two basic characterizations of American religiosity: the enduring popularity of religion, and a seemingly large gap between belonging and acting.[22] Over the past fifty years the United States has had very high rates of church attendance and belief in the importance of religion as compared to other nations in the world. Relatively speaking, religion remains popular in American life. But there are three interrelated gaps between belonging and acting.

## The Ethics Gap

Given the popularity of religion, why is there relatively little evidence of it in societal structures? An obvious answer is that religion and its implications for action in the world seem relegated to Sunday activity. Another answer is that acting upon Christian morality can threaten long-standing American judicial, political, and commercial institutions. Jesse Jackson and Pat Robertson campaigned for the presidency in 1988. Thirty-nine percent of Americans said that it was a bad idea (only 16 percent said it was a good idea, and 41 percent said it made no difference to them). Jerry Falwell's fundamentalist political movement, the Moral Majority, was very active in the 1980 and 1984 presidential election years. The Moral Majority did have an impact on some congressional elections, but by the end of the 1980s Falwell had become one of the most unpopular figures in American life. A more substantive answer to the ethics gap is that Christian denominations have very different interpretations of Christian morality and right action in the world. I suspect that the unpopularity of Falwell and the political failures of Jackson and Robertson may have had as much to do with their interpretation of Christianity and Christian morality as it did with their political platforms.

## The Knowledge Gap

The second gap between religious belonging and acting is the knowledge gap. Most Christians know relatively little about their religion. Between 1954 and 1982 the number of college-educated Americans increased dramatically. Moreover, a majority of Americans had attended Sunday School or its equivalent. Yet, in 1982 only 42 percent of adult Americans knew that Jesus delivered the Sermon on the Mount, an increase of only 8 percent over 1954. Only 46 percent could name all four gospels, an increase of 11 percent. And there was actually a decrease in the percentage of people who knew that Jesus was born in Bethlehem—from 75 percent in 1954 to 70 percent in 1982. I suspect that current percentages would be similar to those of 1982. While knowing these basic Christian facts is not exactly fundamental to Christian faith, lack of knowing points to more substantive problems.

The knowledge gap indicates that the educational level of U.S. adult Christians has increased significantly, but their knowledge of Christianity has not kept pace. This gap is the fault neither of the state educational system nor of private higher education. Christian religious education is not their primary mission. Rather, it is the fault of Christian churches. More than ever before adult Christians have the capacity to understand the historical flow of Christian tradition in its great search for ultimate meaning in life. Christian ministers, however, have tended to ignore that capacity for understanding. All too often preaching is considered the equivalent of education. These are two vastly different activities. Good sermons inspire more than they educate. Sermons should draw upon the common context that good education provides over a long period of time.

Unfortunately, Christian ministry education and formation does not include a significant amount of course work on the principles of adult education. It is not unusual for Catholic seminaries to have only one semester class on the educational aspects of ministry. Protestant ministers often get the message in their seminaries that Christian education is not the heart of their ministry. Christian education has become the province of religious educators—the non-ordained. The educational level of religious educators tends to be less than that of ordained ministers. If their educational level is the same or greater, religious educators often complain that their expertise in religious education is still not taken seriously. No wonder Christian adults tend not to attend classes. Adult religious education methods are often not employed and educational needs assessments are rarely undertaken. Adults respond negatively or indifferently to educational programs that do not meet their needs.

### The Believer Gap

There is a difference between believing and belonging. The mark of a believer is active participation, even if that participation is away from the church itself. For instance, many believers understand that their ministry is in their work place. They raise moral questions in hospitals, corporations, governmental agencies, and the many other places. Other believers find meaning in working or volunteering in the church community. They provide the structure for others to come and worship and participate in church activities. This is not to say that "belongers" are not good people. But the Christian community should encourage belongers to make the step to become believers.

These three gaps are interrelated because they are symptomatic of a basic problem—religious relevancy. The motivation to close those gaps comes from a sense of relevance. How is Christianity and its underlying spirituality relevant to me and society? How can I act upon an ethical or moral code if I do not know the traditions and rationale that underlie it? How can I become a true believer if I am not sure what there is to believe? What does belief have to do with the present concerns of everyday living? These questions should direct the efforts of ministers and religious educators. Churches that give direct, simple answers to these questions are flourishing today. The problem is that many of the answers are simplistic and incomplete. A more thoughtful and honest approach is needed in order for churches to meet their primary purpose for being—bringing their members to mature spirituality.

### RELIGIOUS DISCONTINUITY

The picture of religiosity in American life painted by sociologists, developmentalists, and poll data has both continuity and discontinuity. Attitudes about core religious beliefs have been relatively stable over the past fifty years, and U.S. religiosity, in general, is significantly higher than religiosity in other Western contemporary cultures. Nonetheless, religion in American life is at risk because of the discontinuity between belonging and believing. Most Americans belong to a church, synagogue, or temple, but few of us incorporate our religious beliefs into personal and public action. Religion in the United States is a relatively private affair relegated to subjective experience and vast suspicion. When religion is evoked in political and other public affairs, it is met with a great deal of skepticism. Pat Robertson, Jerry Falwell, and Randall Terry have the political scars to prove it. But religious inaction and skepticism are symptoms of deeper spiritual problems.

Gallup's and Castelli's description of believers is another way of talking about what Fowler describes as faith(ing). Fowler's concept of faith as an active life stance is particularly important for us today. To set one's heart, faithing, is another way of talking about spirituality. Just as faith is deeper and more personal than religion, the same can be said about spirituality. When religion gives organized shape to the natural orientation that we have toward spirituality, then we are more likely to be active participants. Public action based upon mature spirituality is less likely to be met with skepticism because it maintains tolerance for plurality and compassion for others amid the ambiguities of life.

The fact that religious beliefs have remained stable over much of this past century is not necessarily comforting. The typical American's conception of God painted by poll data looks suspiciously like ourselves. Such an image traditionally has been fostered by U.S. mainline Christianity. But God as a "grandfather in the sky" has many limitations for today's culture. First, it gives God a superhuman identity. He seems to be an all-powerful version of us, not the mysterious reality that has preoccupied the thoughts and hopes of human beings since the beginning of time. Even a superhuman identity is too small a concept for God.

Second, this traditional conception of God is exclusively masculine. It indicates that the female half of humanity is less than godlike. As a male it has been hard for me to understand the impact that exclusively male imagery has on females. My wife and daughter have helped me appreciate how benevolent paternalism subtly undermines positive self-image and mature spirituality.

Third, the image conveys that God's home is in the sky, not here with us. It fosters a sense of the temporary nature of our earthly existence. No doubt our existence on earth is temporary, but this image can lead to the impression that earthly existence is something different from spiritual existence. We are *both* earthly and spiritual.

We need many conceptions of God. Any description of God can only be proximate and inadequate. Describing an infinite and mysterious reality within the limited bounds of human language is impossible. We can, however, use imagery that comes from our experience. We can certainly describe God as loving father, if that is part of our spiritual experience of God. But we need to recognize the limitations of that image and open ourselves to other images of God that can be just as true to spiritual experience.

Knowledge of God is not solely a matter of human reason, nor is it devoid of human reason. We will never know God with certainty. Yet, that reality is hard for us to accept. We are left with only a tentative certainty of faith. Mature spirituality embraces that tentativeness. Spiritually mature people are intellectually honest about their faith and make their quest for connection with God part of the drama of everyday living. This search is another way of describing religious literacy. A religiously literate person recognizes the many attempts that Christianity has made to understand God. The more we know about this fascinating story of faith the more we can appreciate the mysterious complexity of the search itself. The inadequacy of simplistic answers to profound questions become all too apparent.

Just as faith as part of the human constitution, so might we describe trust. We all long to be able to trust each other. Clearly, judicial systems and legal systems are poor alternatives to trust among people. And we desire to trust God. Legalistic approaches to religion describe the breakdown in trust among congregation members and with God. In order to trust in God we need to rid ourselves of our intellectual and spiritual dishonesty. Making "deals" with God in our prayer life is one familiar form of dishonesty for most of us. To trust in God's love for us as human beings is so much harder. We need to ask ourselves with all of the intellectual and emotional honesty we can muster, "In whom am I willing to place my ultimate trust?" And we need to act on that trust.

### VOCATION

We have viewed religiosity in the United States from the perspectives of social trend, church affiliation, stages of faith, and religious relevancy. One way of synthesizing these viewpoints is through Fowler's concept of vocation. The term *vocation* often connotes profession or singular direction in life, as in the vocations of education, medicine, law, ministry, vowed religious life, and so forth. In much broader terms, Fowler characterizes vocation as "the response a person makes with his or her total self to the address of God and to the calling to partnership."[23] Vocation, in this sense, is a radically open orientation to God and others. It gives spiritual purpose to leisure, work, private life, and public life. Vocation is our basic orientation to life.

Fowler points out seven consequences to embracing this notion of vocation.[24] First, it rids us of a competitive outlook on life. We are called to excellence within our possibilities. Our vocation is unique and suited to us. Second, a noncompetitive outlook on life frees us from the anxiety of others fulfilling our life dream first. We rest assured that our traveling the path through various stages of life will be at a pace fit for us. There is no single achievement awaiting fulfillment. Third, this outlook on vocation frees us to rejoice in the gifts and talents of others. We participate in an "ecology of giftedness." To be in vocation is to be in community. Each person contributes to the common good from his or her strengths. Fourth, freed from anxiety and envy we do not have to meet the expectations of others—to be all things to all people. Experiencing serious setbacks then becomes a challenge, an opportunity for examination, rather than the debilitating experience of failure. Reaching our limits simply gives contour and organization to life. Fifth, vocation is a gracious balance of time and energy. It is the opposite of drivenness or workaholism. Fulfillment is found in balance. Sixth, vocation frees us from the tyranny of time. In vocation, time is not a depleting commodity. Rather, we live into time. Each period of life, each moment, is reflective of the whole. Seventh, vocation follows the contours of human development. The pattern and focus of listening to the address of God and our relationship with others change over time.

The next chapter describes the quest for certainty and the breakdown of trust that Christian religion in the United States inadvertently has embraced. Much of U.S. Christianity has been involved in the business of promoting certainty in an uncertain world. The world view that supports that approach to religion is termed fundamentalism. Again, we start with stories of faith and then step back a bit to look at an overview of this religious phenomenon. An alternative to religious certainty is presented in Christian spiritual humanism.

# Chapter 3 _____

# A Fundamentalist
# World View

✝

Mike and Susan were happy with their church. They had three children, a boy twelve, and two girls, eight and six years old. Mike had a good job in a manufacturing plant, and Susan worked part-time in a day-care center. They had attended a local Christian church for most of their lives. Their pastor made it clear that the church proudly embraced the label fundamentalist. Susan had grown close to the church over the years, more so than Mike. But they attended as a family every Sunday. Susan kept asking my wife and me to come to their church services. We were happy with our church and declined. Eventually, though, we did accept an invitation to a presentation given by a visiting preacher on what the Bible says about the end of the world. We were curious.

The presentation was given during the Wednesday evening church service. The guest speaker was introduced as a visiting pastor and an expert on the Book of Revelations. He was a large man in a dark navy blue suit that did not quite button. His hair was meticulously combed and sprayed in place. He surveyed the scene from the huge oak pulpit, towering above the congregation. The church was packed with the curious, the devout, and everyone in between.

The entire congregation sat mesmerized by the cadence and logic of the preacher's two-hour presentation. The central message was that the world was coming to an end before the year 2000. The Bible was very clear about this in the Book of Revelations. All of the signs were interpreted, and clear lessons were outlined. Either we would be part of the Rapture, when those who declared Christ as their personal savior would be taken up into heaven together in an instant, or we would stay to suffer the torments of the end of the world. The message had a definite allure. If the end of the world is coming, why save for retirement, why stay in an unrewarding job, why keep your children in public schools that subject them to the drug culture and secular humanism?

Susan bought the message, literally. She bought the tapes and books that were on sale after the service. Mike was skeptical. Susan wanted to move to North Carolina and wait for the Rapture. They would sell their house, quit their jobs, and wait with other believers. My wife and I lost track of them over their months of arguing. Shortly thereafter, we heard that their marriage ended in divorce. No one seemed to know if Susan went to North Carolina. My wife and I often wonder what happened to the children.

Similar preaching and approaches to the Bible are broadcast virtually every day on television. Promises of salvation abound. A few hours of viewing on Christian broadcast channels surface a variety of different religious promises.

An example—With hands raised, the television host opens the television show by belting out an upbeat country gospel song.[1] He soon is joined by his wife for a duet on an elaborate set replete with chandeliers. Both are dressed in rhinestone country wear. Hair styles, cosmetics, and jewelry are extreme. Their message is clear: If you have trouble in your life, "proclaim the Lord Jesus as your Savior." Along with that step, the implication is to contribute money (love offerings) to their television ministry. Long-distance telephone numbers run continuously along the bottom of the television screen for prayer counseling and contributions. Success and extravagance are displayed unabashedly. The implication is that you too can be successful if you follow the tele-evangelists' instructions. The guide, they proclaim, is the Bible. They read and expound upon a few lines between songs. Emotional testimonies are given by people who were successful by worldly standards: an ex-rock star who found the Lord and is now recovering from drug addiction; a successful businessman whose life was saved when he decided against a suicide attempt by watching the show. These witnesses have been saved and are now more successful then ever before!

Tears are a mainstay. At one point the hostess emotionally tells about a mysterious woman who appeared from nowhere to thank her for setting up the television ministry in a foreign country. Before disappearing she gave the hostess a flower. The story ends in an emotional climax as the flower is shown to the viewing audience.

Catholic viewers recognize the implied connection between miraculous appearances of Mary, Jesus' mother, and the woman in the story. The show ends with a song and an appeal for money to spread the television ministry around the world.

The next show on the Christian broadcast channel is very different from the previous one. The host is a large man, dripping with perspiration, but impeccably dressed in a dark blue suit and stylish tie. After a gospel song he admonishes the audience to reject Satan. He scolds liberal preachers and their followers who downplay sin and Satan in the world. "They have given in to this godless society and secular humanism," he proclaims during his ten-minute sermon. He quotes scripture to prove his argument, then moves on to the next song. Choir members, many of whom had tears in their eyes during the sermon, sing forcefully but with restrained rhythm. After the song the host prays with ardent fervor for people with diseases of various types and for others with trouble in their family. The Bible reading and sermon that follow have stern tones. He laments over churches that cater only to the saved and the rich. Tearfully, the preacher looks into the camera and tells his viewers, "This church is for us sinners, and you know in your heart that you are a sinner." He bellows with raised eyebrows, "Get Satan out of your dirty life and let God clean it up." Then, with eyes closed, his preaching takes on a staccato beat. Logic leaves, but words flow nonetheless as his body moves rhythmically back and forth. The show ends with an announcer inviting viewers to call the 800 number on the television screen to receive "Offer #802, Bible Readings for the Lonely."

A click of the remote control to another television channel finds yet another style of Christian ministry show. In a television studio with stained glass in the background and a book stand to the left, a young-looking Catholic monk attired in full habit—brown robe and hood with a hugh rosary wrapped around him— sits in a chair facing the camera. There is no music or choir. The monk talks to the viewer about the decline of values in American family life and the increase in sexual promiscuity. His message today is especially for Catholics. "The vocation of a Catholic is to be obedient to Holy Mother Church," he implores. His logic is that the pope, as successor to St. Peter, and the Catholic hierarchy are entrusted with the truth of Jesus Christ. If U.S. Catholics would obey official church teachings they would be a leaven, an effective influence on the rest of the culture. He quotes the Bible and Catholic doctrine regarding sexual norms. His voice rises and he becomes flushed, saying: "Catholic theologians, and yes, some parish priests, are confusing the faithful with theological speculation. They interpret doctrine according to their own opinion and on their own terms." He outlines his argument in a twenty-minute sermon, then punctuates his closing remarks with a muted slam of his fist on the podium, speaking forcefully: "The Ten Commandments are not the 'Ten Suggestions,' and the Catholic church is not a democracy! The holy father does not take opinion polls to make up his mind. Be faithful to the holy father or leave the church. There is no room for 'cafeteria Catholics,' who pick and choose only what they want to believe." A small paperback book on sexual morality is offered by an announcer at the end of the show along with an address and an 800 number.

Common to these television shows is an underlying outlook on life and religion—fundamentalism. Fundamentalism appears in many forms and venues of American life. In order to understand fundamentalism and its impact on U.S. culture, it is necessary to understand its antagonism to modern culture. Fundamentalism finds greatest expression in its fight against secular humanism.

## THE FUNDAMENTALIST FIGHT AGAINST MODERNISM

Fundamentalism arose in reaction to modernism of the late nineteenth century. The modernist position, especially in its extreme, indeed, is a challenge to religion. Modernist philosophy contends that we can make our way in life and discover the secrets of the universe and human existence solely through science, reason, and human cooperation. Fundamentalists claim that liberal ministers and religious scholars read the Bible through the lens of evolutionary theories of human origins as well as through philosophical systems that replace traditional norms and doctrines.[2] These religious liberals, according to fundamentalists, have given in to the lure of modernism.

### Modernism

Origins of modernism are to be found in the Enlightenment tradition. Bruce Lawrence contends that Immanuel Kant and August Comte were among the more important bearers of Enlightenment thought.[3] Kant (1724–1804) viewed reason and unlimited human potential as superior to religious dogmatism. In his philosophy, Kant supplanted trust in the mysteries of revealed religion, and the professional classes of clergymen who perpetuated them, with trust in the ethical conduct of human beings in society as the basis for universal law. For Kant, practical reason and ethical conduct represent limitless human potential; institutional religion, with its age-old superstitions, represents a limiting of human potential. Kant, in effect, argued that ethical conduct should not depend upon religion; rather, religion should depend upon ethical conduct. Thus, Kant did not abandon religion altogether. He gave precedence to ethical duty driven by the dictates of practical reason over conceptions of revealed religious doctrine. Kant's philosophy spoke to the concerns of his era. He gave a philosophical system for the pursuit of human ethical conduct. While many philosophers after Kant did not agree with him, most felt a need to respond to his principles. Schleiermacher, Hegel, Feuerbach, Comte, and later, Nietzsche, Marx, and Freud helped to shape the post-Kantian period and contributed to the foundations of modernist philosophy—secular humanism.[4]

Unlike Kant, Auguste Comte (1798–1857) sought to displace religion as a source of values in nineteenth-century Europe.[5] Comte, a founder of sociology as a discipline, was a philosophical positivist and religious nihilist. Comte's positivism rejected abstract theoretical speculation about the intellect and society. He contended that such speculation needed to be tested with the scientific method. Comte's nihilist position sought to replace religion with science as the source of social values. He equated religion with childhood, and philosophy and science with adulthood. In the first stage of Comte's schema, the theological, human beings understand themselves and the world around them as controlled by the supernatural. In the second stage, the philosophical, speculation on abstract causes and forces determines reality. In the third stage, positive science, human beings use science to observe facts and data and determine relationships among them. Thus, for Comte, both individual and social progress depend upon religion's being displaced by philosophy and positive science. Comte looked to the natural sciences as examples of how society should evolve.

Enlightenment philosophy as embodied in modernism had little impact on the average person in the nineteenth century.[6] The publication of Charles Darwin's On the Origin of Species by Means of Natural Selection in 1859, however, captivated public imagination. Darwin did not originate the idea of evolution. Philosophers from before the Christian period and up to Darwin's era had proposed a number of different ways in which plants and animals evolve over time. But Darwin's work galvanized religious opinion and became a lightning rod for religious-secular debate.

Darwin's principle of natural selection proposes that simple organisms evolve into more complex forms over time by means of variations that better ensure survival. He believed that successful variations could be inherited and thus lead to new species. His theory accounted for biological variations and changes in the location of species, and it set the groundwork for explanation of periods of great variation and great stability in the long cycle of time.

Controversies invariably arise when Darwin's theory is applied to the human species. It contradicts a literal interpretation of biblical creation narratives in which species (including human beings) are presumed to have been created in basically the same form in which they currently exist. An implication of Darwin's theory is that species do not evolve in an orderly manner from an original creation point. Rather, species emerge, evolve, and disappear at different times based upon environmental circumstances. If human beings were not created "as is," then how has Homo sapiens evolved as a species? Fundamentalists look to the Bible for answers. Modernists look to science.

Another Enlightenment development that has affected the average person is in the realm of society and politics. Comte, Emile Durkheim (1858–1917), and others helped give a modernist philosophical and sociological rationale to the French and American revolutions. Both revolutions claimed that human freedom and individual rights take precedence over social class and religion. It is the dignity of the human person that undergirds the guarantees of the U.S. Constitution, not social standing or religious affiliation. The separation of church and state in the United States articulates this principle. Moral and ethical conduct are valued above church affiliation. All churches are welcome in the United States if they conform with accepted standards of ethical conduct. In a sense, Kant's call for ethical conduct to supplant religion is being at least partially realized in the American experiment. One way in which fundamentalists fight back against this modernist victory is through their efforts to return prayer to the public schools.

Religious perspectives on human behavior have become supplanted by another Enlightenment development—psychoanalysis. Freud and his followers, as well as psychotherapists of varying schools of thought, depict the human psyche as reacting to genetic, cognitive, environmental, and social factors in life. Looking into the depths of consciousness takes courage and time. In many respects, psychoanalytic theories countermand traditional notions of the role of Satan and sinful impulses in human behavior. "The devil made me do it," was a plausible statement in the eighteenth century, but it is now the punch line to jokes in the twentieth century.

The psychoanalyst's couch has replaced the confessional, and in the minds of some people, therapists have replaced ministers.

A most telling indicator of a modernist mindset is the application of scientific principles to the Bible.[7] Nineteenth-century German scholars in particular pioneered the use of critical tools such as literary form criticism, history, and archeology to examine scripture. Resulting exegesis rocked the religious world. The scholarly consensus that the Pentateuch, the first five books of the Bible, was not written until the eighth century B.C.E. attacked the common religious sense about the Bible. Moreover, that analysis contradicts that possibility of Moses' authorship of the Pentateuch—a scandalous proposition in the minds of many. All of scripture had become fair game for scientific inquiry. With the rise of critical biblical scholarship, the search for the historical Jesus had begun.

Given this type of analysis, a literal interpretation of scripture is unthinkable to the modern world view. Most modern scholars grapple with meanings that underlie the gospels, prayers, myths, and other literary genres that constitute the Bible. This type of biblical criticism challenges traditional notions of authorship, context, and purpose. Most scripture scholars from the nineteenth century on have not been trying to disprove the Bible. Rather, they search for religious meaning in the original context in which the scriptures were written. The tools of modern science are used to understand better the revelatory nature of the Bible. Fundamentalists view this scholarship as nothing less than an attack on biblical truth by backsliders and academic agnostics.

Contemporary biblical scholars utilize the hermeneutical sciences to interpret scripture as a sacred text that can speak to contemporary culture, thereby distinguishing it from secular historical texts. The nuances of hermeneutics, however, are lost on the average person. For most people, biblical revelation boils down to whether or not God said it in the Bible.

Historical scholarship on church history also affects modern consciousness. Under the critical eye of historical analysis, the insights and vagaries that characterize church history relativize church structure and polity. If theology and church structures were not always the way they are today, that history calls the current situation into question. Modernist approaches to history also are inclined to replace God as director of this great historical drama with the human beings directing their own drama. Religious modernists may indeed subscribe to a belief in God as the First Mover of creation, but they also contend that human beings have created their own destiny through decisions of their own free will. Thus, they consider the possibility of a predestined fate for human history as utterly remote. Modernists of a religious ilk, or otherwise, place importance in historical consciousness. Fundamentalists find little use for either conservative or subversive perspectives on history because of a thoroughgoing belief in God's plan for humanity.

Historian Nancy T. Ammerman notes two particular expressions of modernism in Christianity.[8] The first, a sociopolitical expression, is the Social Gospel movement of the early twentieth century. That movement rejected exclusive emphasis on saving the souls of individuals in favor of political democracy, world peace movements, and efforts to end racial and social discrimination. The Enlightenment tradition's optimism about the ability of human beings to order society for the benefit of all was embraced by some ministers and Christian laity. Gospel values gave theological weight to the quest for justice. The doctrine of postmillennialism, which claims that a thousand years of righteous living in society will bring about the return of Christ, was espoused.

The second expression, theological in nature, is relativity. Christian modernists question Christianity's uniqueness, especially in terms of salvation expectations, and place an emphasis on comparative-religion scholarship. Modern scripture scholarship undermines the idea that the Bible is uniquely the word of God. Study of other ancient religions reveals striking similarities with biblical literature. Whether creation stories, flood stories, virgin births, or resurrections, oral traditions coming from different cultures and religions point to the possibility of multiple connections with the divine. Comparative-religion scholars analyze the human need for religiosity and how that need is fulfilled by the sacred texts, doctrines, and practices of religion in general. Religion, in this view, affects culture, and culture affects religion. Engaging in this type of scholarship makes it difficult to claim that salvation is found solely in one religion or denomination.

The foregoing brief indicators of a modernist world view are far from complete, but they give a sense of the broad shift in cultural understanding that Americans have experienced. A good description of modernism is found in Marty's and Appleby's *Fundamentalism Observed*: "Modern cultures include at least three dimensions uncongenial to fundamentalists: a preference for secular rationality; the adoption of religious tolerance with accompanying tendencies toward relativism; and individualism."[9] Most Americans see no problem with this picture of modern culture. The American psyche has

become so ingrained with secular rationality, tendencies toward relativism, and individualism that most Americans identify these characteristics as virtues rather than vices. Most U.S. citizens like to
think of themselves as reasonable individuals who are accepting of
other people's religious beliefs. Thus, most Americans find it hard to
criticize these dimensions of modernism. Fundamentalists, on the
other hand, feel compelled not only to criticize them but to fight
against them.

Historian Bruce Lawrence's description of modernism sounds a
bit more stinging. He contends that

> modernism is the search for individual autonomy driven by a
> set of socially encoded values emphasizing change over conti-
> nuity; quantity over quality; efficient production, power, and
> profit over sympathy for traditional values or vocations, in both
> the public and private spheres. At its utopian extreme, it en-
> thrones one economic strategy, consumer-oriented capitalism,
> as the surest means to technological progress that will also
> eliminate social unrest and physical discomfort.[10]

The search for individual autonomy can be a desperate quest for
identity in a pluralistic culture. Change certainly is the norm for
American cultural life. Materialism does promote quantity over quality.
"Getting lean and mean" expresses corporate efficiency, often at the
expense of traditional values and understandings of vocation. Con-
sumer-oriented capitalism can be seen as a social technology—a
social Darwinism—ensuring that the "most fit to succeed" have the
opportunity to do so and that the "less fit" are given the opportunity
to succeed with jobs provided by the "most fit."

Liberals and conservatives take pause over different elements of
these descriptions of cultural modernism. There are elements of
American modern culture that need correction and adjustment,
whether we term them modernist or not. Most Americans agree with
some of the elements of the fundamentalist fight against modern
culture. But American Christian fundamentalists will not accept partial allegiance to their cause.

### Protestant Fundamentalism in America

Modern biblical scholarship took root in late nineteenth-century
American Protestantism.[11] Liberal Protestant ministers were seeking ways to accommodate Christianity with the new science and
modern world. There was hardly consensus, however, about the
need to accommodate religion with modern culture. Protestant conservatives held to traditional beliefs about the Bible and revelation

despite liberal Protestant demythologizing tendencies. In addition to holding traditional conservative beliefs, Evangelical Protestants placed great emphasis on the need to be "born again" into a personal relationship with Jesus. Being born again can mean a private statement of commitment or a public baptism or an open statement at a religious service.

Fundamentalist beliefs first were articulated with the publication of a series of twelve pamphlets published between 1910 and 1915 and titled *The Fundamentals*. Nancy T. Ammerman describes how fundamentalism got its name: " In 1920 Curtis Lee Laws, editor of the Northern Baptist newspaper *The Watchman Examiner*, wrote that a 'fundamentalist' is a person willing to 'do battle royal' for the fundamentals of the faith. It was both a description and a call to action, and the name stuck."[12] U.S. fundamentalist beliefs are generally characterized by four features: evangelism, inerrancy, dispensational premillennialism, and separatism.

*Evangelism.* The compulsion to evangelize comes from the importance that fundamentalists place in "being saved." If being saved is the sure way to heaven, then it is incumbent upon the "saved" to bring Jesus Christ to the "lost." Fundamentalist television and radio broadcasts, print materials, street preaching, and door-to-door visiting attest to evangelistic fervor. Not all evangelists, however, are comfortable with the fundamentalist label. Billy Graham and other Christian conservatives feel more comfortable being described as Evangelical. While both Evangelicals and fundamentalists are orthodox conservatives, Evangelicals take a less aggressive and antagonistic stance toward society.

*Inerrancy.* Fundamentalists believe in an inerrant interpretation of the Bible. In other words, no part of the Bible can be in error. If one part of the Bible is wrong, then it is not the word of God. The Bible is taken literally even in historical and scientific matters. To bolster the inerrancy argument, three rational proofs of inerrancy were formulated in the late nineteenth century. In order for the Bible to be wrong a critic would have to prove that the passage in dispute was part of the original biblical text, that it means what the critic says it means, and that it can be proven to be wrong by science.[13] This defense is impenetrable because, first, even the earliest biblical texts can be deemed translations subject to human error. Second, the critic can be attacked on the basis of misinterpretation. Third, science does not work on absolute certainty; hypotheses need to be open to continued testing. In effect, these rational proofs rest on the interpretation and authority of the fundamentalist defenders. According to this rationale, the fundamentalist authority figure cannot be wrong.

The most famous instance of the defense of biblical inerrancy in the United States was the 1925 Scopes trial decision in Tennessee, which led to a ban on teaching evolution theory in the public schools of Tennessee, Arkansas, and Mississippi.[14] Clarence Darrow won the hearts of the country in his defense of modern science. But William Jennings Bryan won the trial. The ban against teaching evolution in those school systems held for forty-three years until a 1968 Supreme Court decision overturned it. The issue reappeared in a failed 1982 attempt to have the Supreme Court order that "scientific creationism" be allowed in public schools as an alternative to the theory of evolution.

*Dispensational Premillennialism.* A third characteristic of fundamentalist belief, dispensational premillennialism, means that salvation will be dispensed to Christian faithful at the Coming of Christ prior to the millennium (the thousand-year reign of Christ). For dispensationalists, history is divided into periods—dispensations— in which God grants salvation in different ways. The current dispensation was begun by Jesus and is continued by the Christian church until the beginning of the millennium. Premillennialists believe that Christ will return at the beginning of the millennium (as opposed to postmillennialists, who believe that Christ will return at the end of the millennium). Premillennialists look forward to the Rapture, in which the Christian faithful will disappear in an instant as they rise to heaven with Christ. A popular fundamentalist bumper sticker reads, "This car will be unoccupied at the Rapture." These beliefs emanate from an interpretation of Matthew 24 and 1 Thessalonians 4 as well as from apocalyptic literature in both the Old Testament and New Testament. It also is common practice for fundamentalist preachers to interpret the highly symbolic writing in the Book of Revelation according to current world events as a way of predicting the Rapture.

*Separatism.* A fourth characteristic, separatism, is a matter of uniformity. Dissenting opinions are not tolerated by fundamentalists; their primary value is uniformity of belief and practice. Consequently, their uniformity clearly distinguishes the fundamentalist community from other churches or movements. For this reason, fundamentalist churches tend to be independent of mainline Protestantism. Charismatic leaders, almost exclusively male, shepherd their fundamentalist congregations according to straightforward rules of belief and conduct. There is no room for "backsliding," nor is there a desire to engage in ecumenical relations with other churches. The true expression of faith and salvation is to be found only within fundamentalism.

## Fundamentalist Separatism and Activism

As fundamentalism started to mature in the twentieth century, two distinct expressions emerged: the separatists and the activists.[15] Separatists believe that being born again is enough for the true believer to be prepared for the coming of Christ. Social transformation of the culture is hopeless because of the tight grip that Satan has upon the world. Things will only get worse before the Rapture. Bob Jones III and the pastors of many small churches are good examples of fundamentalist separatists. Activists, on the other hand, believe that it is their duty to be as active as possible in politics, public education, and other social institutions in order to be faithful to their rebirth in Christ. Jerry Falwell represents the activist type of fundamentalist. His now defunct Moral Majority was an effort to infuse fundamentalism into mainstream American politics. Another example of fundamentalist activism is Operation Rescue, an interdenominational antiabortion organization. Operation Rescue's aggressive abortion clinic protests have become commonplace news events. Randall Terry, its leader, clearly operates out of a fundamentalist framework. He unabashedly proclaims himself an evangelist seeking to save souls for Christ. Fundamentalist activists have a significant position in the political Religious Right.

## Catholic Traditionalism in America

A Catholic expression of fundamentalism is found in traditionalism.[16] The variety of expression that characterizes Protestant fundamentalism is also found in Catholic traditionalism. Contemporary Catholic conservatives belong to groups such as Catholics United in the Faith (CUF), Opus Dei, The Blue Army, and Mother Angelica's Eternal Word Television Network (EWTN). There is a mix of conservative and traditionalist principles and practices in all of these groups. A primary example of a strict traditionalist movement is that of French bishop Marcel Lefebvre, who defied the pope and other magisterial leaders by refusing to switch from the Latin Mass to Mass in the language of the people. He also characterized most of the Vatican Council II (1962–65) reforms as apostasy. His separatist movement is a classic expression of traditionalism.

While not all of these traditionalist groups fit the characteristics of fundamentalism, there are similar tendencies: " . . . highly cognitive-doctrinal religiosity marked by objectivism, dogmatism, and literalism. Traditionalist ideology is also exclusivist and elitist, separatist in its action orientation, and deeply imbued with a conspiracy sense of social causality. The Traditionalist ideology also manifests clear affinities with many right-wing political orientations."[17]

Dinges further contends that traditionalism is a religious protest against the spreading of false doctrine. The reforms generated by Vatican Council II and the dissent that followed promulgation of the papal encyclical *Humanae Vitae* are proximate targets of traditionalist protest. According to Andrew Greeley, the promulgation of *Humane Vitae* (1968) by Pope Paul VI was a watershed moment for U.S. Catholics.[18] In that encyclical the pope affirmed the traditional view that only natural means of birth control are allowed. This teaching runs contrary to the common sense of most U.S. Catholics. In fact, the majority of the pope's advisors on the matter were in favor of accepting artificial means of birth control. But Pope Paul VI refused to break with the church's tradition that the purpose of sexual intercourse is primarily reproduction. Catholic traditionalists view adherence to this encyclical as a test of faithfulness to the pope and Catholicism in general.

A primary purpose of Vatican Council II was an updating of church life to meet the challenges of the modern world. The reforms that came out of that council, therefore, are seen by Catholic traditionalists as accommodations to modern culture. Such reforms as ecumenical outreach, lay ministry, liturgical reform, and so forth are scandalous to traditionalists. They believe that the whole deposit of truth is found in the Catholic church and that the Catholic church was literally founded by Jesus Christ. Protestants are viewed, therefore, as misled.

Catholic liberals and progressives use Vatican Council II as a rudder for direction on contemporary church teachings. Catholic traditionalists, on the other hand, use the Council of Trent (1545–63) and Vatican Council I (1869–70) as their rudders. The Council of Trent, convened in reaction to the Protestant Reformation, instituted major reforms in the Catholic church's institutional structure, more clearly defined doctrine, commissioned an official translation of scripture, instituted religious education in the form of a catechism, and initiated liturgical reform.

Vatican Council I met under Pope Pius IX's direction to confront the modern world's challenges to religious orthodoxy and authority. Democracy, socialism, the industrial revolution, and modern philosophical thought were seen as threats to longstanding conceptions of the church's hierarchical authority. The doctrine of papal infallibility was instituted during this council to ensure continuity of religious authority in the spiritual realm. Before the end of the council, nationalistic Italian troops were threatening to take over the Vatican. In the eyes of the pope and the bishops, the temporal world was in chaos.

Both the Council of Trent and Vatican I, therefore, were reactions to cultural attitudes about religion and challenges to church authority. The world view of Catholic traditionalists is formed in large part by the legacy of these councils. Contemporary traditionalists perceive that modernist thought has infiltrated Catholic theology and that the world is in or near chaos. They consider the pope, bishops, and priests (in that order) protectors of Catholic tradition. When that protection seems lax, Catholic traditionalists react fiercely. Traditionalist groups vary greatly in their relationship with the hierarchy. Some Catholic groups with traditionalist tendencies do not hesitate to attack publicly the character of a bishop whom they view as modernist. Others pay deference to bishops and other magisterial leaders by privately trying to persuade them to change their views.

Most traditionalist groups consider lay people in pastoral or religious education positions "fair game" for verbal attack. A favorite tactic is to report these lay ministers to the Vatican and the local bishop for supposedly unorthodox views and teaching. Traditionalist groups also have been known to take notes during sermons for the purpose of reporting parish priests whom they consider unorthodox.

*Contemporary Catholic Traditionalism.* The tradition that contemporary U.S. Catholic traditionalists refer to is basically Catholic church life from 1900 to 1965. Even given the rhetoric about faithfulness to tradition, most traditionalists are either misinformed about church history or selectively focus on particular eras as being primary—such as the Council of Trent and Vatican I periods. Practically speaking, however, most traditionalists view tradition as the beliefs and practices emphasized in the previous generation.

Contemporary Catholic traditionalists pine especially for the Catholic identity of the 1945 to 1965 era. The great waves of European Catholic immigrants had subsided and an indigenous U.S. Catholicism had taken root. This was a time of religious popularity in general, and Catholicism had a very distinctive identity based upon its longstanding sense of being a religious minority in the United States and from beliefs and practices inherited from Trent and Vatican I. The election of John F. Kennedy was a watershed moment. At last a Catholic could become president, an impossible scenario only a few decades earlier. But cultural success had its price. Now considered mainstream, Catholic identity was becoming indistinguishable from American identity.

This conservative era seemingly fell apart with the initiatives of Vatican Council II. The Latin Mass was changed to the language of the people, with the presider facing the people instead of facing the altar. Abstaining from eating meat on Fridays moved from a requirement (under pain of mortal sin) to a suggestion. Classification of mortal and venial sins was deemphasized in favor of making a fundamental option of living in faithful witness to God. Religious priests, brothers, and sisters started leaving their orders in great numbers in the decade after the council; the current priest shortage is rooted in that time period. The hard-won respect and stability that characterized Catholicism in the late 1950s to mid-1960s seemed to have fallen with cultural success. Catholic traditionalists view this change as modernism's inroads into Catholicism; Catholic liberals view it as reform. In either case, the search for Catholic identity is still underway.

## Fundamentalism: A Summary Description

Marty and Appleby describe fundamentalism as "a habit of mind and a pattern of behavior found within modern religious communities and embodied in certain representative individuals and movements. Fundamentalism is, in other words, a religious way of being that manifests itself as a strategy by which beleaguered believers attempt to preserve their distinctive identity as a people or group."[19] A distinction can be made, then, between fundamentalism as a movement and as a world view. Each fundamentalist movement or cluster of movements has its own unique social and theological history. But they all have common characteristics. Fundamentalism is not a return to religious origins. It is a reaction to a perceived attack on religion by modern culture. Fundamentalism is an attempt to assert the fundamentals of faith in order to cure the ills of a secularized society. A primary problem with a fundamentalist world view is that the fundamentals chosen tend *not* to be fundamental to faith and that fundamentalism constantly fights against contemporary culture without trying to understand it in the light of faith.

A fundamentalist world view is found in movements within almost all religions. Fundamentalists believe that their religious identity is being threatened by contemporary culture, and the fierceness of the fundamentalist argument arises from their sense of loss and betrayal. Most fundamentalist movements begin as reactions to the perceived effects of modernity within church communities rather than to movements outside of churches. Modern scripture scholarship and the promotion of historical consciousness about religious tradition heighten the need for self-critique and change, which are very threatening for fundamentalists.

Despite fundamentalist rhetoric, fundamentalism does not conserve religious tradition. Rather, fundamentalists arm themselves with a selected set of doctrines and practices from the past that they rearticulate and retrofit for their cultural wars. Thus, fundamentalist movements are as modern as the culture with which they do battle. Fundamentalists do not shy away from using the technological tools of the modern world, for example, mass media and computers. Their critique of modernity is rather selective.

Fundamentalists are locked in a battle with modernism, and to a certain extent, they are correct to be suspicious. The typical modernist did naively expect that religion would decline in culture and humanity would be freed from the slavery of religious dogmatism and enlightened by scientific method and social progress. The dedicated modernist of the late nineteenth century did not expect religion to be around as we enter the twenty-first century.

While fundamentalists fight for what they perceive as the fundamentals of their religion, Marty and Appleby contend that their choice of those fundamentals tends to be dictated by three interrelated motivations: (1) the choice to scandalize (to shock); (2) the need for absolute authority; and (3) the will to rule.[20] I suggest an additional motivation—privatized (rather than communal) religiosity. These motivations, combined with the perception of being besieged by modern culture, an inclination to fight back against that culture, a need to preserve their religious identity, a tendency toward literalism and dualism, and a remarkable sense of resilience and inventiveness, are important elements of the fundamentalist world view.

*Shock Treatment.* The choice to scandalize is important for fundamentalists because they view contemporary culture as secularized and anti-Christian. Suspicion of education and of cultural sophistication drives this motivation. In other words, they feel the need to shock the culture into realizing the evil of its ways. "God said it [in the Bible], I believe it, that's all I need to know" is a common Protestant fundamentalist refrain. "God said it [through church tradition], I believe it, that's all I need to know" is the Catholic equivalent. It is no accident that fundamentalists concentrate on miracles, the mysteries of faith, spiritual healing, the devil, and other concepts and events that challenge contemporary culture. These aspects of religion are shocking to the modern mindset.

*Absolute Authority.* The second motivation, a need for absolute authority, is a search for certainty in a very uncertain world. There is comfort in being told what is absolutely right or wrong in our pluralistic and confusing age. Adherence to absolute authority minimizes the need for personal grappling with complex life issues. It also easily identifies those who are uncertain about the need for absolute authority, the "fence-sitters," and attempts to force a commitment of religious allegiance.

Fundamentalists target liberals. The liberal, according to fundamentalists, is one who pushes the modernist agenda. The liberal becomes a foil, a stereotype, that fundamentalists can name as one who advocates a supposedly failed modernist agenda—secularization, big government, feminism, and social experiments of all sorts that have eroded (according to fundamentalists) the moral fabric of society. Liberals, according to fundamentalists, promote relativism. Fundamentalists believe that the primary way to fight relativism is through the promotion of clear and absolute authority.

*The Will to Rule.* The third motivation, the will to rule, accounts for rather mean-spirited attacks by fundamentalists upon those who disagree with them; those who wish to rule tend not to enter into conversation. They justify the need to exert power over others in terms of helping them save their souls. This need also is fueled by eschatology (the study of end times) and justified militancy. A primary fundamentalist principle is that secularized modern culture is hastening the end of the world, at which time the elect (believers) will be vindicated. A variety of premillennial expectations fuel the sense of urgency for fundamentalist principles to dominate culture for the culture's own good. Fundamentalist objectives for society are viewed as imperatives. They need to be implemented, even if doing so requires coercion or force. Aligning with the elect, in this fundamentalist world view, sets boundaries and the need to declare oneself. Such boundary setting occurs more efficiently when directed by clearly defined authority figures.

*Privatized Religiosity.* The fourth motivation, privatized religiosity, promotes exclusive religiosity at the expense of communal religiosity. Although thousands of fundamentalists gather at conferences and religious events, the primary focus is on personal prayer, saving one's soul, and how to save the souls of others. Fundamentalism in religion is akin to individualism in culture. Yet, at the same time, fundamentalist groups provide very strong community life. The "us against them" stance galvanizes the fundamentalist community. The closeness and exclusiveness of the community dissociates the fundamentalist community from other communities within their religion and from the larger culture.

Even though many fundamentalist groups seem to have developed a social conscience over the past decade, a primary motivation for such outreach is evangelization. Conversion is viewed as a means of getting to heaven—"getting right with God." The problem is that "getting right" means getting the right answers and practices from the fundamentalist group. Little room is left for a social view of Christianity that works for justice. This does not mean that fundamentalists are heartless or that they are not interested in social problems, but that they tend to place more emphasis upon charity rather than the promotion of just social systems. Fundamentalists have very little trust in the ability of social systems to be just. Righteousness, they believe, is to be found in their movement.

### A Fundamentalistic World View

While knowledge of fundamentalist movements in the late nineteenth century and the twentieth century helps us understand contemporary fundamentalism, a more important insight is found in the fundamentalist world view. This world view is found in more Christian churches than the ones in the formal movements that claim the name. For this reason the term *fundamentalistic* better describes this world view.

A fundamentalistic world view is composed in part of ahistorical consciousness or selective historical consciousness, a dualistic understanding of the sacred and the secular, a belligerent stance toward the present cultural and religious situation, a literalist interpretation of the Bible, and an apocalyptic vision of the future. Religion, in this world view, functions as a vehicle for obtaining absolute truth from religious authorities for the purpose of obtaining salvation. Personal motivations for subscribing to this view of religion include a fear of ambiguity; anxiety about cultural conspiracies threatening religious orthodoxy; a privatized sense of salvation; longing for a closely knit, like-minded community; and the need to discover a new beginning in life (being born again).

Characteristics of this fundamentalistic world view are found throughout Christian churches. An integrated sense of Christian history is rarely heard from pulpits and is seldom the focus of adult Sunday School and religious education classes. Historical consciousness is feared by too many clergy and laity. "Too much knowledge leads to confusion among the people," is a common excuse. An equally unsatisfactory perspective is a selective approach to history. For instance, the Reformation might be the only period to which church education refers, or the first century of Christianity, or the first half of the twentieth century.

Many Christian churches promote a sacred-secular dualism, a perspective that is regrettably understandable. Whether by conscious choice or not, many pastors set up contemporary culture as a foil for their sermons. The implied message is that God is to be found in the church, not in the world. Yet, most people in the congregation know that many good things occur in the popular culture despite all of its ills. They know many holy people who do not attend their church. This cognitive and spiritual dissonance separates that which is sacred (God) from life. A fundamentalistic world view embraces this dualism with the tight grip of certainty in a righteous God who will save only the saved.

Religious belligerence is an apt description for a fundamentalistic world view. It is much easier to fight for a closely held religious conviction than to attempt to understand another point of view. Too often the tendency is to rush to argument without first engaging in conversation. Religious belligerence becomes vicious with character assassination or physical harm. The only goal of interaction is conversion, not understanding.

Literalism is a fundamentalistic trademark. A literal interpretation of the Bible is a substitute for the hard work of reading scripture in its context. The irony is that a literal interpretation of the Bible is itself an exercise in interpretation. In effect, preachers read a passage from scripture and interpret it by their explanation of what God is saying to us. The literalist believes that interpretation comes directly from the Bible and not from tradition, much less from modern biblical scholarship. The implication is that preachers or pastors are immune to misinterpretation because the Holy Spirit somehow is whispering the truth in their ear.

A fundamentalistic world view promotes endism.[21] Predictions about the end of the world fuel the urgency of evangelistic fire. As the song goes, "I want to be in that number when the saints go marching in [to heaven]." Periodic predictions about the end of the world have come and gone. But the anxiety and uncertainty of life makes yet the next prediction plausible to many.

Fear of ambiguity is pervasive in Christian churches of all denominations. Most Christians feel that the stakes are too high not to be sure of religious answers to the ultimate questions of life. Certainty gives answers; ambiguity gives questions. Yet most Christian theologians and mystics understand God to be a mystery to be lived into; they term the God of certainty as idolatrous. Yet, too many pastors preach certainty to pacify the anxieties of their church members.

A fundamentalistic world view is disposed to conspiracy theories. Whether it is the Trilateral Commission, a conspiracy of liberal clergy trying to undermine religious orthodoxy, an atheistic communist threat, the liberal media, or secular humanistic higher education, this world view takes them all very seriously. A "Christ against culture" stance toward life characterizes a fundamentalistic mindset. This religious mindset understands a primary purpose of Christianity as constant battle with contemporary culture.[22] Cultural obstructions to a Christian-ordered society, God's plan for the world, are seen as evil, if not satanic.

"Are you saved?" is a very important question for a person with this world view. Often, however, this concern about salvation is privatized into a closely knit fundamentalistic community. Asking the question "Are *we* saved?" makes sense only in the context of that community. It is tantamount to asking whether you are one with the group, which reinforces the need to belong in a like-minded church community. Salvation then becomes a function of membership in the sense of subscribing to the tenets of that community. New life, being born again, is a badge to be worn proudly. Whether through baptism of water or conviction, this symbol of commitment is a sign of membership in the elect—those who will be ready for Christ's return.

## Positive Contributions of Fundamentalism

At age fifteen Rita found herself drifting away from her parents and her long-time circle of friends. Until she confided in one friend, Jennifer, she told no one about the sexual abuse she endured at the hands of her grandfather. Rage and self-hatred boiled within her. She was often physically sick from the drugs that Jennifer gave her. The drugs numbed the pain and, at the same time, alienated her from everyone she loved. She was on a fast track to self-destruction.

The overdose almost ended it all. Brad, one of the school's "Jesus freaks," found her passed out in the schoolyard and called for help just in time to save her life. Her parents could not believe this was happening. They loved and cared for her as best they could given the commitments of their busy lives. Both of them were professionals. They tried to provide the best education they could find for their children and gave positive reinforcement at home. Given their hectic lifestyle, they felt fortunate to have their parents close at hand to care for Rita and her younger brother. But something had gone terribly wrong.

The story of Rita's abuse finally came out in counseling sessions after the hospital stay. Rita's parents were in shock. How could her grandfather do such a monstrous thing? It could not be true. He vehemently denied everything, claiming, "The poor child is having delusions from the drugs." Because the abuse happened five years earlier, it was hard to prove. But Rita's older cousin knew the truth. The same thing happened to her when she was nine years old. The grandfather finally agreed to enter a counseling program when Rita's parents threatened a criminal law suit.

Brad regularly visited Rita in the hospital, but he did not know the full story. She still felt lost, like a torn rag doll that no one wanted, despite her parents' obvious love and care for her. Brad invited her to his church's youth-group meetings. Rita declined the first few invitations but eventually accepted his invitation to a church social. Then she started attending the youth-group meetings. In a small-group session during a meeting Rita told her story. Amid the tears, she was embraced by all.

Rita started attending the church with Brad and his family every Wednesday evening and Sunday morning. This was a "full gospel" church that proudly proclaimed itself as fundamentalist. Rita's parents were confused by it all. They were not church-going people. They believed in God and tried to treat other people fairly, but they could not accept the fundamentalist principles that Rita started to espouse. Nevertheless, they supported her decision to be baptized.

Rita has enrolled in a church-related university and is preparing for a career in nursing. She and Brad plan to marry after college. His family considers Rita part of the family. Through her religion Rita has found meaning and structure in life amid a very confusing world. Evil is a very real concept to her. She believes that her grandfather succumbed to the evil that pervades a culture filled with pornography and sexual permissiveness. She also believes that the drug culture is a manifestation of satanic impulses. She has not alienated herself from her parents, but she prays for her parents' conversion to her church's vision of life. For the moment, they do not talk about religion at home. Her hope is that they will accept her new religion.

Despite problems associated with both fundamentalist religious movements and, more broadly, the principles of a fundamentalistic world view, fundamentalism has made positive contributions to contemporary culture. Fundamentalists dare to take a stand on religious issues and to act upon their convictions. They seek to transform

U.S. culture for the better. A deep sense of commitment keeps their fight alive. Whether or not one agrees with the principles of the political Religious Right, this conglomeration of movements has brought religious values into public discourse. The abortion pickets orchestrated by Randall Terry and Operation Rescue are reminiscent of Civil Rights marches of the early 1960s and the Vietnam War protests of the latter part of that same decade.

Fundamentalism provides a form of community within a culture of individualism. The attempt to organize around deeply held religious convictions takes commitment and community formation skills. These communities often provide the only structure for many people to approach the ultimate questions of life. In some cases these communities provide a way out of a life of drug addiction and other forms of destructive behavior, as well as a refuge from the evils of modern life.

Fundamentalist cautions about placing complete trust in secular rationality can be helpful. The popularity about spirituality among natural scientists today attests to the limits of the scientific method. Scientists from Albert Einstein to Carl Sagan to Brian Swimme attest to the limits of conventional rationality in explaining the universe. There must be room for the possibility of having revealed religion as a conversation partner in cultural discourse. Fundamentalists make it their business to have their voices heard.

# CHRISTIAN SPIRITUAL HUMANISM

## AN ALTERNATIVE WORLD VIEW

Tim had never been a very religious person. People were shocked to hear him say so, though, because he constantly went out of his way to help other people. Tim always had had heavy suspicions about organized religion. His attitude came from his parents, who had bad experiences of church when they were young. His mother talked about being excluded from social events because she did not belong to the "right" church in the small town in which she grew up. It was not that she was not invited to be a member. The very active young minister in charge of evangelism was certain that his church was the way to religious and social success. It was just that she was not attracted to the church, and she resented being pressured. So she endured the exclusion with a sense of rebellious pride.

Tim's father never believed the fire-and-brimstone sermons of his uncle, the preacher. He compared his uncle's words with his actions and decided early on that religious people were hypocritical. Tim's father had a rather cynical view of life in general. Despite this negative view of religion, Tim's parents went out of their way to help people in need. They did so out of compassion. Tim followed their example and studied social work in college. It was there that his suspicions about religion became firmly established. In studying psychology, counseling, and sociology he saw the potential for organized religion's "spiritual and psychic abuse," as one of his professors put it. After graduation Tim became a social worker in a small city in Mississippi.

Tim married Lucy two weeks after he started his job. Her parents did not like the small church they attended, but they attended nevertheless. Lucy, also a social worker, said that her family attended out of social obligation and fear of hell. "You never know," her mother used to say, "that crazy old preacher may be right. I'm not taking any chances. Giving a couple of hours a week to God won't kill you, and it's the right thing to do."

When their son was an infant, Tim and Lucy took turns getting up in the middle of the night with him. Tim watched the late-night evangelists when it was his turn. It was not that he went out of his way to find them. While channel surfing he would stop and listen to what the preachers had to say. At first the crass commercialism of TV religion only confirmed his distrust. But as he watched he realized that he too was searching for something deeper in life.

Lucy's pregnancy and the birth of their son, Charles, were the springboard for her spiritual quest. The nurse who led the natural childbirth class that she and Tim attended also conducted classes in New Age spirituality. Tim immediately felt uncomfortable at these sessions and soon dropped out. But Lucy liked them. She attended throughout her pregnancy but stopped after Charles's birth. There seemed to be too little time.

Charles's birth seemed like a miracle to Tim and Lucy. He led them to consider their spiritual lives.

"In what religion should we raise him?" asked Tim.

"Maybe we shouldn't raise him in any organized religion," Lucy responded. "We should trust in our own spiritual instincts and raise him according to what we believe about God in our hearts."

"But what if we're wrong? It's all guesswork for us," Tim responded. "Maybe the Bible has answers to our questions. Maybe it's just preachers and church people who are the problem. Let's start reading the Bible ourselves."

Their Bible reading lasted two weeks. They eventually enrolled Charles in a Christian day-care center, but Tim and Lucy never joined a church.

## CHRISTIAN SPIRITUAL HUMANISM

There are millions of people like Tim and Lucy, people who want to have faith in something greater than themselves. Most Christian churches want to reach out to them. Evangelism is an important part of their mission. A primary problem is that the world of the Tims and Lucys in the United States is much different from the world of many church ministers and members. Too many ministers view evangelism as bringing faith to people rather than helping people discover how faith is a natural part of what it means to be human. People already have faith; they need help in making sense out of it and testing it against faith that has been handed down for thousands of years. Christian religion has what people need, a faith tradition that can be a resource for today. While our questions may be somewhat different from those of centuries past, we are not the first generation to have the ultimate questions of life. There are answers, or at least a process for finding those answers, in Christian tradition.

The previous chapter outlined how a fundamentalistic world view pervades much of Christian church life in the United States. Despite some positive contributions to U.S. culture, a fundamentalistic world view fulfills the spiritual needs of only a small percentage of Americans. For most, it tends to retard adult spirituality.

Fundamentalism need not lay exclusive claim to getting back to the fundamentals of faith. Another way of getting back to the fundamentals can be described as determining what is vital to faith and spirituality rather than waging a pointless battle with modernism. In many ways U.S. culture has moved beyond the modern period to what increasingly is being described as the postmodern period. No doubt postmodern culture has many ills and is in need of redemption. But fundamentalism has little chance of promoting that redemption. An alternative world view, Christian spiritual humanism, does have a chance because it provides reasonable and responsible ways to deepen spirituality. It promotes the choice to understand, the need for taking personal responsibility for one's decisions, the will to share power with others, an emphasis on communal religiosity, historical consciousness, religious holism, a cultural critique, biblical scholarship, and a constructive vision of the future.

## Understanding

Christian spiritual humanism affirms the need for Christianity to make a difference in the world, which means at times to be counter-cultural. Thus Christian spiritual humanists and fundamentalists have similar intentions for the transformation of culture. Christian spiritual humanism seeks to do just that and, at the same time, provides a context for greater understanding of religion; a mature spirituality; and a chance to make a positive, long-term impact on U.S. culture. *Understanding* does not imply total acceptance of contemporary culture. Rather, it means that religious people need to understand that truth can be found in the many ways that human beings find religious meaning in their lives. While total acceptance is not possible or desirable, understanding other religious meanings may enrich our own religious tradition. For example, many Christians involved in Jewish-Christian dialogue find insights into the Jewishness of Jesus that enrich their understanding of Christian spirituality.

## Personal Responsibility

Personal responsibility for religious decision-making is far harder than simply obeying rules set by others. Despite claims to the contrary, adhering to absolute authority is rarely practiced by fundamentalists. When some fundamentalists disagree with a person in authority, their allegiance simply shifts to another authority figure more in line with their beliefs. Many Roman Catholic traditionalists engage in this practice by disagreeing with their bishop in favor of the opinion of other bishops. Likewise, many Protestant fundamentalists change churches when the pastor does not espouse their notions of the fundamentals.

Adherence to absolute authority sounds like the mark of a true believer. But often such dedication amounts to avoidance of taking personal responsibility for the consequences of our actions. Personal responsibility means informing our conscience with the moral imperatives of Christian belief and practice and filtering those norms through personal experience and the concrete situation to determine the most loving thing to do.[1] Personal responsibility means accepting the consequences of our decisions and actions, rather than shifting the responsibility from one authority figure to another.

## Power with Others

Power is a crucial element to both fundamentalistic and Christian spiritual humanist world views. The fundamentalistic motivation—the will to rule—attempts to enforce notions about absolute truth and to determine who subscribes to it and who does not. Boundaries are clearly set. A Christian spiritual humanist view of power, however, does not set such definitive boundaries. Power rests in the truth of ideas and practices to which a religious community subscribes. "You will know them by their deeds" speaks to a communal sense of power. Christian spiritual humanist power comes from the common sense of the community without the requirement of rigid declarations of devotion. There is the freedom to move in and out of these faith communities. Individual freedom of conscience is upheld in the context of a community of faith. People belong to these communities because they find religious meaning in them, not because they fear damnation.

This type of power springs from a people of faith participating in a living religious tradition that tolerates differences of opinion but also requires a critical evaluation of all such differences. Fundamentalists might term such communities relativist; Christian spiritual humanists call them related, that is, people in faith relationship.[2]

### Communal Religiosity

Just as power with others leads to a communal sense of power, communal religiosity is an experience of spiritual solidarity. Privatized spirituality is an outgrowth of privatized religious community. Churches that alienate themselves from the rest of the world tend to create a hot house atmosphere in which one's spirituality supposedly grows only within the confines of the church. This fundamentalistic view of spirituality privatizes religiosity. Communal religiosity comes from churches that nurture the spirituality of their members through theological reflection, prayer, and practices intended to explore the sacred. That exploration extends throughout the culture and the earth. Churches that embrace communal religiosity grow through the nurturing of their members without making the members dependent upon the church. Communal religiosity gives a basis for integrating religion into the member's whole life. Privatized religiosity tends to segment religion into the church's perspective on life. Communal religiosity enables engagement with culture. Privatized religiosity disables interaction with culture because it demonizes culture.

### Historical Consciousness

Does knowledge of history lead to freedom? Fundamentalists would tend to say, "No, knowledge of everlasting truth leads to freedom." Christian spiritual humanists would be inclined to answer, "History helps us to understand the paths to truth." Historical consciousness comes from engagement with history. A Christian spiritual humanist world view values knowledge of the ebb and flow of history. Learning from the mistakes of the past does lead to greater freedom. Consequences of individual decisions and, even more so, large cultural decisions are not immediately evident. The results of decisions become clearer with the passage of time and attention to the study of history.

History gives perspective to current understandings about truth. An idealized sense of how we inherit current understandings about religious truth, or any other form of truth, for that matter, is not help-ful. History often reveals philosophical, political, and economic fac-tors that have affected the formulation of the religious doctrine that we have inherited.

A Christian spiritual humanist view of history invites participation in the flow of history. Becoming knowledgeable about a religious tradition, for example, engenders in us a sense of ownership. The more history we know about a tradition, the more likely we are to retell the story. A feeling of belonging, of being an insider, comes from being able to tell the story. Knowledge of history also gives us a good sense of which voices have shaped history and which voices have been left out of the main story line. It is often said that history is written by the victors. Insight can be gained from the losers—from those whose perspectives were initially rejected. Some of the most respected theologians of the Christian era were initially rejected, in-cluding St. Thomas Aquinas. History places the contemporary situ-ation into perspective.

## A Cultural Critique

Criticizing someone or something can mean to castigate, censure, or disparage. This sense is found in the fundamentalistic view of culture. A Christian spiritual humanist view offers its critique in a more constructive vein; its intent is to analyze, examine, probe, or study the culture. The first instinct for the Christian spiritual human-ist should be to try to understand why human beings do what they do. Despite a significant hunger for spirituality, why does a signifi-cant part of the population find little meaning in regular church at-tendance? A constructive critique of this cultural situation does not start with the premise that the culture is secularized, antireligious, and evil. Rather, constructive critique investigates *why* such people find little meaning in regular church attendance. Both church prac-tice and cultural habits are investigated. Church and culture are con-nected in a web of meanings that need mutual understanding in or-der to progress.

## Biblical Scholarship

Biblical literalism and biblical scholarship belong in different world views. A fundamentalistic view of the Bible is an attempt to preserve God's revelation as eternal truth. If any part of the Bible is viewed as errant (untrue) or inconsistent, then God's word is inconsistent. And that is not possible, since God is eternally consistent in God's own truth.

Biblical scholarship proceeds from a much different starting point. It is not necessary that all elements of the Bible are inerrant or consistent. The Bible, according to most biblical scholars, is a remarkable collection of different forms of literature that proclaim God's revelation at a particular time and place. Truth is to be found in the meaning that comes to us in light of understanding in our context. Revelation, then, is ongoing, as we take that truth and try to understand its implications in our time and place. The Bible compels us to look for God's revelation in our living tradition—the Spirit with us in our lives and in the world around us. It moves us from the vivid imagery of its pages to imagine a world with God in it.

### Constructive Vision

An apocalyptic vision of the future (endism), so characteristic of a fundamentalistic world view, is seductive. It often becomes a form of religious escapism, in which we believe that God will lift us up and out of a world gone bad. Our responsibility, in this view, is to "get saved" and to save others. Thus social and ecological responsibility become less important.

Constructive vision, on the other hand, takes seriously God's mandate to care for each other. Jesus preached about the Reign of God as the fulfillment of the command to love God and each other. Christianity is meant to make a difference in the world. Constructive vision means being in the struggle for the "long haul." We find dignity in grappling with sin and injustice, not in witnessing the victory.

### Religious Holism

Religious dualism pervades a fundamentalistic world view. Religious holism, in a Christian spiritual humanist world view, is the integration of our religious experience with our whole life, an attempt to recognize the sacred in everyday experience. The Christian spiritual humanist views emotions, imagination, prayer life, and intellect as entry points to the sacred; they need to be integrated into a consistent stance toward life. At times, especially in moments of crisis, emotion gives sacred insight. When the fabric of daily existence is torn by the tragic or inexplicable, we turn to God for wisdom and solace. Religious imagination also comes from intuition and mystical experience. The mystics break through the seemingly impossible or the paradoxical with spiritual wisdom. Prayer can be an experience of God on a plane different from everyday experience. However we come to our religious experience, it is important to be intellectually honest about what we believe. Such honesty is a mark of mature spirituality. We are constantly trying to make sense out of our lives. We need to understand our religious experience as much as possible so that we can act upon it in responsible ways.

Salvation, in a Christian spiritual humanist world view, is found in the relationship among God, ourselves, and others. The proximate ground of that embrace is the earth; the more expansive location is the universe. "Others" means more than other human beings; the web of life includes all of creation, creatures of every variety. Science and religion are coming together in a recognition of the ecological connections between the earth, life of all sorts, and the cosmos.[3] Some scientists are talking like mystics; some theologians are talking like scientists. These interdisciplinary efforts are making it possible for more and more people to believe that we live in a sacred cosmos.

Religion, in a Christian spiritual humanist world view, functions as a vehicle for approaching truth in a holistic way in a pluralistic, uncertain world; it hopes to forge a relationship with God and all of creation. Personal motivations for subscribing to this view of religion are not far removed from those of a fundamentalistic view of religion; fear of ambiguity, anxiety about threats to religious orthodoxy, questions about salvation, longing for community, and the need for a new beginning are still present. The difference is that a Christian spiritual humanist view of religion struggles with those fears in a church community that is open to the God of religious tradition and God's presence in the world. A Christian spiritual humanist is part of a vibrant living tradition that seeks the growth in the Spirit of God to be found in all creation.

A primary and natural way of exposing adults to a spiritual humanist world view of religion is through adult Christian religious education. But far too many adult religious education classes fall into the trap of a fundamentalist world view that fails to promote adult spirituality. Such educational programs characterize culture as almost completely secularized and corrupt, focus upon the need for absolute authority, strive to protect their religious power base, and emphasize personal religiosity. As a result, most people will not attend or will soon drift away. It is time for Christian churches to provide alternatives.

# Chapter 5 _____

# EDUCATION OF THE PUBLIC

✟

The story appeared in an inconspicuous section of the newspaper under the headline "Student Stabbed in School Fight." Lucille read it to herself as if it were about someone else's son. She could not believe that it had happened to Jarrel. "I guess things are so bad that school stabbings are reported on the front page only if the victim dies," she thought, her face tightening as the words formed in her mind. The tears were gone and anger was taking hold. "Thank God Jarrel is all right," she thought, as she tried to assure herself. The doctors in the emergency room confirmed that vital organs appeared to be undamaged. Jarrel was not going to die, at least not that afternoon. But she knew that the wounds would have long-term effects.

The fight was about the usual thing—respect—a precious commodity in the inner city. Jarrel was the victim of William, a twenty-year-old tenth-grader. William had been in and out of school all of his life, mostly out. This year was his last chance to stay in a regular school. If this did not work out, he would have to enroll in G.E.D. classes. "All I want to do is play football," William told his friends. "You can't do that in no G.E.D. classes." William was out of shape. His gut was heading down to the waist, and years of alcohol and drugs were making their mark on his face. Yet William had an outrageously enticing smile that seemed to erase those ugly lines.

William was a force to contend with. His teachers suspected that he had a fairly high I.Q. He had little interest in school other than sports. William had gotten off to a bad start. His mother did not enroll him in kindergarten. She was too busy trying to survive with a low-paying job, four kids, no husband, and a huge thirst for alcohol. William was the youngest child and the only male in the house. His three sisters were all out of school. Two of them got pregnant in high school and now had their own babies. The fathers took no responsibility for the children. The sister closest in age to William, Lynette, was the only one who had graduated from high school. She spent two years at the local college and found a good job in the suburbs. Lynette eventually found an apartment close to her job and rarely came home. She and her sisters were not on speaking terms. William's grandmother and his aunt with her three children lived in the other half of the duplex. His grandmother, Mildred, kept things together. A tall, regal woman, she was active in the church three blocks away. Mildred made sure that the children went to church. She arranged for William to start school, even if it was a late start. But he never caught up. William failed the sixth and eighth grades due to lack of attendance and fighting. When he failed the ninth grade, Mildred said that she could not do anything more with him. By this time he had two arrests for petty theft, for which he received probation. Mildred wanted nothing more to do with him, except that she would still pray for him and wait for him to come back, on her terms.

William's grandfather had passed away before he was born. He had a civil service job of some sort and was a deacon in the church. William never knew his father, and that always bothered him. His mother said that his father had been in and out of the house, but by the time William was born, he was out completely. William's mother said that she was sure that he was dead from drugs. Nobody could survive the way he took drugs. If the drugs didn't kill him the pushers would.

Most of William's friends did not know their fathers very well either. It seemed normal. William's life was on the street. He grew up there. His time at home was spent eating, sleeping, and watching a blaring television set. He stopped going to church with his mother and grandmother when he was ten years old because his friends were teasing him too much. He preferred to endure his grandmother's wrath.

Alcohol and drugs were always a part of William's life, but his passion was football. He played on the city playground teams and on and off in school, although his grades prevented him from playing much of the time.

William could not remember ever studying at home. He depended upon his good memory, and when he attended class, he passed. Attendance, however, was not his strong suit. William would often skip school but attend football practice in the afternoon. This was against school policy, but the football coaches didn't pay much attention to such rules so long as the student was passing. William tried to stay in school during football season. He wanted football to be his ticket out of the ghetto.

It was the spring semester of the tenth grade when William attacked Jarrel. The confrontation was unusual for Jarrel. He usually could avoid a fight. Jarrel was six feet five inches tall with enough weight to play tight end. But Jarrel was not coordinated enough to be a good athlete. He was sure of this and did not try out for the varsity team, despite telephone calls from the coaches. Before his father left for good, when Jarrel was in the fifth grade, he told Jarrel to keep trying, that the coordination would come later. "Just be aggressive, you're big enough to just run people over," his father said with a grin. "If I had your size, I'd be in the pros." In his heart Jarrel knew that he would never be good enough to be in the pros. His mother, Betty, made sure of that. In many different ways, she let him know that education was his way to success. Betty had worked hard to become a nurse, and it was paying off. She and Jarrel lived in a reasonably safe neighborhood just outside of the housing project. It was not the best, but it was a mansion compared to the project she grew up in.

William's and Jarrel's high school principal, Mr. Richardson, was coasting. As he put it in his brooding moments, the youthful idealism of his early years in education had been snuffed out by inner city politics, apathy, and an atmosphere of incompetence. This was a rationalization, and he knew it. But it was too close to being true for him to care. Mr. Richardson followed school board policy, no more, no less. He had been sued twice: first, by the parent of a disruptive student who actually was psychotic; and second, for sexual harassment by a vengeful, incompetent teacher whom he had disciplined. He was eight years away from retirement. Trapped in a stressful job, he was afraid to leave and afraid to continue. Mr. Richardson was the first administrator to reach the scene of the fight.

The fight started after two weeks of harassment by William. Jarrel, a senior and class president, was a good target. He was high profile and big, but William was sure that he would not fight. William accused Jarrel of being gay. Jarrel just ignored him, which was what William hated most. William's friends got great pleasure in spreading the rumor that Jarrel wouldn't fight William because his accusation was true.

Jarrel was in no mood for William's tormenting on the day of the fight. He had just received his second letter notifying him that he was accepted to a college but did not qualify for an academic scholarship. His high school grades were exceptional, but his SAT scores were low. They didn't say anything, but the college admissions counselors almost rolled their eyes when they saw the name of his high school. Good grades from this school meant that you could read. Jarrel was in no mood to be messed with.

William caught up with Jarrel in the middle of a crowded school hall. Just as he began to start his usual harassment Jarrel swung around and moved toward a surprised William. Jarrel was a good seven inches taller than William, and the full impact of his size was felt by William and everyone else as Jarrel hovered over him, only inches away. Jarrel said in a voice loud enough for everyone to hear, "Tell your boyfriends that I'm not gay. But even if I were, you still would be shining my shoes ten years from now, assuming you don't overdose, Boy." The hall exploded with laughter as William stood stunned. His friends were laughing too and pointing at him. As his rage surged, he instinctively pulled the knife from his pocket. He slashed at Jarrel's face with full force, missing but then swinging back and connecting with a thrust to the lower back. As Jarrel crumbled to the floor in bloody anguish, William ran.

Mr. Richardson had just reached the end of the hall when the laughter turned to screams. William was running directly toward him with fear frozen on his face. Mr. Richardson reached out to grab him but pulled back at the last moment. William dodged to the right but lost his balance and crashed into the tiled wall. The next thing he knew he was in a hospital emergency room with an intern looking down at him. Two police officers stood next to her.

## THE PROBLEM WITH EDUCATION

Everyone seems to be an expert on education. Whether at school board meetings, parent-teacher conferences, in corporate board rooms, or on talk radio, most adults speak eloquently about what is wrong with education. Most often, such talk is uninformed. We tend to think about education in terms of the education that we have received. Getting back to the basics in education, for most of us, means getting back to our own school background. But experiences of education vary greatly; education may have many different purposes and methods. Liberal arts education is very different from technical education. Traditional models of teaching and learning are very different from progressive methods. Education in a small school is different from that in a large school. Large research universities are different from liberal arts colleges. Two teachers in the same school, teaching the same subject, can have different approaches. The educational experience of students in those classrooms, therefore, will be very different. Too often the term *education* is assumed to mean the same thing for everyone. Clearly, it means different things to different people.

## AN EDUCATIONAL ECOLOGY

There is another reason why talk about education often is misinformed. When most adults think about education, they mean schooling. No doubt schools are the most intentional educational institutions in contemporary U.S. culture. Yet education is much more. Historian of education Bernard Bailyn claims that education is a way in which a culture transmits itself from one generation to the next.[1] In researching the origins of contemporary U.S. education from the mid-seventeenth century to the mid-nineteenth century, he identifies education as coming from four primary cultural institutions: family, school, church, and apprenticeship. These institutions worked in tandem with each other during that time period.[2] Schools were small by today's standards and were viewed as an extension of the family. Churches also were closely tied to family. The church provided moral guidance for both family affairs and civil affairs. An impetus for schooling was the need to become literate enough to read the Bible, the centerpiece of early schooling. Apprenticeship was the early equivalent of on-the-job training and technical education. But apprenticeship was more than that; it was like being accepted into an extended family. Most shops and trades were family operations. Thus, families and churches, in this early period of the U.S. experiment, were the primary educational institutions. Today's situation is much different. Families are in trouble. Divorce rates hover around 50 percent, and usually both spouses work full-time jobs outside of the home. U.S. education today tends not to be anchored by the family. It should be, but that is just not the case.

Historian of education Lawrence Cremin also recognizes the reduction of family influence in education. But he insists that there still exists an ecology of institutions that educate today: households, mass communications, work places, schools, churches, governmental agencies, and other social institutions.[3] In other words, the four educational institutions of the early period of U.S. history have been replaced by many other social institutions. These institutions vary greatly in the intentionality of their educating, but education takes place nonetheless. The totality of an individual's education is the result of the interdependent education received from these social institutions.

### Five Features of Education

Cremin defines education as "the deliberate, systematic, and aimed effort to transmit, evoke, or acquire knowledge, attitudes, values, skills, and sensibilities, as well as any outcomes of that effort."[4] At first glance, Cremin's definition seems a bit complicated and as broad as life itself. But with closer examination, it identifies specific dimensions of education. Five distinctive features are highlighted in his description of education.[5]

*Intentional.* First, the definition stresses intentionality. It distinguishes education from learning that takes place in the course of everyday living. This notion of education makes room for intentional self-education as well as instruction. It also distinguishes home schooling from less intentional aspects of education in the family.

*Generational.* Second, his definition has implications for education across generations. Adults teach children. But sometimes children teach adults, as in immigrant families learning English or teenagers educating their parents about computers.

*Societal.* Third, the definition recognizes that education occurs in society both within and outside of schooling. Parents, peers, siblings, and friends educate one another. Whether engaging in sports on an amateur or professional basis, on-the-job education, hobbies, or interest groups, education takes place all the time. Many different teaching methods and educational strategies are employed in these cultural institutional settings. They often compete with or influence each other. The enormous power of television is now used in classroom instruction. Self-help groups and other types of small-group movements are recognized as effective ways of educating in churches.

Even though there is an ecology of education, it does not mean that all of these social institutions work in tandem. The values of popular television shows often conflict with family values and church values. Corporate values periodically clash with governmental/political values. Family values sometimes contradict values presented in schools. And mass media rival schooling and family as the primary educational institution. Obvious examples of childhood education are *Sesame Street, The Magic School Bus,* and *Barney.* Adult equivalents are *The Learning Channel, The History Channel,* and *Mind Extension University.* These programs intentionally communicate information and values in the process of trying to entertain.

Even in formal classrooms lines are blurred between education and entertainment. Good teachers know how to captivate their students.

Television shows shape attitudes about sexuality, fairness, politics, and many other cultural perspectives. The potency of television is of grave concern to religious groups. They recognize its power to convey attitudes and values to the popular culture. Promotion of consumerism, promiscuity, and antireligious attitudes provokes common complaints.

Similar types of instructional potency exist in other forms of mass media. Newspapers have a long tradition of informing the general public, and in many ways, newspaper organizations understand themselves as educative. They take pride in giving more in-depth information than other forms of mass media. Investigative reporting can be a remarkable form of public education. Broadcast radio is a powerful educational forum as well. Talk-radio entertainer Rush Limbaugh jokingly (and sometimes not so jokingly) describes his call-in radio show as an institute of conservative thought. He prides himself on being able to give mini-lectures (monologues) on the meaning behind the news. He indirectly takes credit for helping shape contemporary U.S. conservatism with occasional inferences about his influence and access to national conservative political figures. At other times he describes himself as simply responding to the groundswell of public opinion and conservative attitudes. But he derides people who suggest that he has a lot of power as a result of his talk show's popularity, with listeners counted in the millions. He condemns the "liberal media" for influencing public opinion by interpreting current events with a big government, socialistic slant. Limbaugh's radio show points to the complexity of education and its intimate connection with values and human growth. Rush's supporters claim that he is educating the public about the dangers of blindly following a liberal social agenda in politics and mass media. In their eyes, he is conserving tried-and-true principles of public morality. His critics describe him as an entertainer who is making a lot of money pandering to fears about the uncertainties of a fast-changing U.S. culture. Depending upon one's perception of politics and morality, he is either a great mass media educator or a very successful demagogue. Whether educator or demagogue (or something in between), one cannot deny his power and influence on popular culture and politics in the 1990s.

*Outcomes.* Fourth, education, according to Cremin's definition, produces both intended and unintended outcomes. The distinctive feature of education, however, is intended outcomes. People can learn a great deal from earthquakes, hurricanes, and other natural phenomena, but terming such activity education makes education so broad that it loses any distinction from life in general. Too broad a definition blurs the intentional learning that occurs. Education involves systematic planning to influence thinking, behavior, and sensibilities. Even though good education allows for the emergence of the unexpected, the serendipitous, there is a plan for the educational experience. This plan may be loosely defined, but it can be described as a curriculum, a course. The course may lead to proficiency in algebra or knowledge about a particular historical period of history or proficiency in repairing a computer. The prescribed direction is laid out, and the process and content are designed to accomplish an educational outcome. Thus, while Cremin's definition of education covers a vast scope of educational activity in culture, it also maintains distinctions between intentional educational settings and more generalized learning in life.

*Paideia.* Fifth, Cremin's definition also recognizes the value-laden aspect of education, the connection between a culture's self-understanding and its transmission. This self-understanding, a vision of life itself as deliberate cultural and ethical aspiration, is the substance and character of a culture, a *paideia*. *Paideia*—the Greek term for raising children—over the centuries has come to mean education. For example, Mortimer Adler's book *The Paideia Proposal* proposes a Great Books type of classical education for all U.S. children as the primary way of introducing them to the great ideas and debates of Western civilization.[6] Professional education and technical education, he proposes, should come after that broad type of education. Problems arise, however, when one tries to select the particular great books used to identify the great ideas. Moreover, this type of proposal underestimates the diversity and pluralism of contemporary U.S. culture. Cremin's use of the term *paideia* does not presume a Great Books curriculum but simply recognizes that education takes place throughout U.S. culture, and it occurs throughout our lives.

Cremin's use of *paideia* includes the ever growing and changing content, values, and aspirations that a culture passes on to each succeeding generation and the process it uses to do so. *Paideia* has individual and social implications. Just as individuals maintain a certain set of values and aspirations, so does a culture. For most of us, education ordinarily begins with the nurturing of certain knowledge, values, attitudes, and behaviors in the family, extended family, and some form of church and school education. Through individual educational histories each member of society enters maturity with a particular lifestyle comprising individual selective accommodations to the meanings and values he or she has learned.

Schooling, for instance, presents us with many meanings and encourages us to take control of our own meaning-making—our world view. In the very early grades we are educated in what it means to interact with a social group outside of the family and we begin learning the symbolic structures of society. For example, language, math, and social studies tell us who we are and what society should be. Ideally, as we move through the elementary and secondary grades, the skills of meaning-making are fine-tuned in tandem with our physical and intellectual development. Higher education builds upon this foundation and deepens this meaning-making activity to the extent of our ability to utilize knowledge and meaning-making in broad ways. Likewise, vocational and on-the-job education presents the knowledge and values that commercial institutions want instilled in their employees. Effective on-the-job education also encourages creativity among employees for self-fulfillment needs and the ongoing development of the corporation. Similarly, U.S. political institutions continually educate teenagers and adults about the value of voting and getting involved in the political system. Political progress also depends upon adults who question distortions in the political process and work for political reform.

An important aspect of individual educational histories in society is the effect that educational efforts bear upon educators or, more broadly, upon the collective self-understanding of society. Just as individuals form a set of meanings and values as they develop and mature, so does a culture. Cultural self-understanding is a concept that is hard to evaluate in our own era, yet we all recognize fundamental differences between U.S. culture in the 1990s and in the 1950s. Schools are different. Many now are unsafe. Corporations are different. Corporate loyalty and employee longevity are not valued as much as they were in the 1950s. In the 1990s the people of the United States are struggling with what it means to be a pluralistic culture. In the 1950s the melting-pot theory of enculturation (a single, unified culture) was the norm.

Education, therefore, involves a process of interaction between individuals and social institutions in the culture. Individuals strive to make sense out of their lives while being influenced by various educational institutions of society. These institutions help guide this process in a mix of complementary and conflicting meanings and values. Social institutions intentionally present meaning and value to us through their educational endeavors. Social institutions, however, are not social machines. They are organized and managed by people. The educational processes of these institutions affect the people in the institutions as much as they affect people in the popular culture.

### Schools as Social Barometers

The current back-to-basics movement in education is a recognition of the failure of public education over the past thirty years. Standardized test scores in public schools remain a concern. Inner-city schools now have metal detectors to prevent guns and knives from being brought to school. Debate rages about the moral and religious implications of providing condoms to students in order to counter the rise in teenage pregnancy or of teaching religiously based sexual abstinence before marriage to prevent the spread of AIDS. Violence-prevention programs attempt to counter the propensity to solve problems with fist fights or more deadly forms of conflict.

Great hope is placed in the ability of schools to cure social ills. That hope, however, is misplaced. Schools clearly reflect the social and cultural conditions of their community. Schools are barometers of the health of the community in which they are located. If inner-city schools are in shambles, it is because inner cities are in shambles. Violence exists in those schools because of the violent culture in the inner city. Inner-city social institutions are in disarray because inner-city families and economic life are falling apart. Change needs to take place in *all* of the social institutions in troubled communities in order for education to be effective.

Schools are also barometers of the health of U.S. culture as a whole. Communities expect more of teachers than of other members of society. At the same time, there is a prevalent lack of respect for teachers captured by George Bernard Shaw's often quoted satirical phrase, "He who can does. He who cannot teaches."[7] The implication is that the teaching profession is for those people who cannot make it in the real world. Moreover, elementary school teachers traditionally have been predominantly women, who have labored under the burden of lower salaries than their male counterparts. Consequently, teachers and school administrators tend to have an "us against them" attitude—teachers against the popular culture. For these reasons teachers and administrators resist accountability in many public school systems. The public blames teachers for failing schools, and teachers blame the local community for lack of support. Nonetheless, schools can make a difference in the lives of children and teenagers. Whether the difference is positive does not depend solely upon teachers and schools, however. School reform depends upon the commitment of local communities and society as a whole—the ecology of social institutions.

EDUCATION OF THE PUBLIC

One of the most thoroughly American and influential philosophers of education in the United States was John Dewey (1859–1952). His writing on philosophy and education was prolific. Why, then, do not Dewey schools abound in the United States? The reason is that Dewey's philosophy of education became identified with the very broadly defined and often discredited Progressive education movement. Progressivism became a catchword for almost any educational approach that reacted against the traditional subject-matter-dominated curriculum. This traditional approach tends to view learners as passive vessels into which knowledge is poured (or forced into) for the learner's own good. Dewey challenged this view of education by promoting the idea that learners need to discover how to reflect critically upon their experience as well as on the subject matter presented to them.

The most succinct statement of Dewey's educational philosophy is "My Pedagogic Creed."[8] Titling his statement a creed rather than a philosophy indicates the moral force he proposes for education. In his creed Dewey describes education as a process in which an individual participates in the social consciousness of a society. It is the duty of educators to enable children to develop as individuals and to do so with the full understanding that they are part of society. As social individuals we all have the responsibility of contributing to the moral good of society to the best of our ability. Dewey understood the school as a social community in which students should learn how to live within a community. This idea of schooling counters an "ivory tower" notion that schools prepare children to live in society after they graduate. And it counters the idea that educators live in an unreal, idealistic world. For Dewey, schools should be models of living during the educational process. In school, students learn how to develop intellectually and to live morally in society. The subject matter of schooling should be presented in such a way that students learn the funded capital of cultural tradition in an active way.

Dewey's philosophy suggests that all of life has scientific, aesthetic, and cultural dimensions, and many ways of communication. School curricula should resist disjointing these disciplines as much as possible because, in truth, all of these dimensions of education are needed by people in any profession. Very early in the twentieth century Dewey pleaded for holistic education in a world of increasing specialization. Dewey lived through the transition of America from an agrarian society to an industrial society. He witnessed the breakdown of small-town life and the emergence of city life. Dewey wanted schools to be places in which children could experience community amid city life.

Dewey claims that education involves the continuing reconstruction of experience and that the process and goal of education is human growth.[9] By "reconstruction" he means that human beings grow through problem-solving experiences by use of reflective thought. He contends that we are constantly reconstructing our experience. Education helps us to learn from our experience in more intentional ways and through the use of greater resources. For these reasons we call adults mature or immature based upon whether or not they have learned from their experience. Human growth, then, is the product of reflected-upon experience. "Growth toward what?" one might ask. Dewey would respond, "More growth." In other words, when we define the product or end of human growth, we become deterministic. We do not know the limits of human potential.

### Miseducation

In Dewey's educational framework there is the possibility of *mis*education. Miseducation retards human growth. It prevents people from developing to their fullest human potential. Unfortunately, instances of miseducation are all too frequent in contemporary society. Again we might look to inner-city schools for an example. School buildings in scandalous conditions of disrepair, poorly prepared or unsupported teachers, and a violent atmosphere all contribute to the miseducation of inner-city children. These children are being treated as if they do not count for much in society, as though they are disposable. It should be no surprise when they act accordingly by striking back against society. Yet, some inner-city schools are exceptions. Parents, teachers, and administrators who overcome a lack or misuse of funds and mediocrity create an oasis of human development amid a culture of despair. These brave souls are educators in an environment of miseducation. This is in no way to suggest that miseducation is confined to inner-city schools. They provide, however, striking examples.

An important aspect of Dewey's philosophy is his emphasis on the continuity or interaction of experience rather than a dualistic view of experience. Examples of seeming dualism include mind and body, means and ends, objectivity and subjectivity, the individual and society, theory and practice, and so forth. But we cannot relate to our mind other than as bodily creatures. Means have as many consequences as the ends they serve. The way we go about problem solving often shapes the outcomes. Objective reality has subjective assumptions that help shape it; the more one probes the assumptions upon which objective reality rests the less objective they become. Thomas Kuhn, philosopher of science, points out that scientific revolutions come from individuals who break out of the existing scientific paradigm (a comprehensive set of assumptions) to create a new one.[10] Human beings are as social as they are individual. It is naive to suggest that we are not, in part, shaped by our language and our communities. Likewise, communities are made of individuals who can alter the community— be they a Hitler or a Ghandi. Theory often directs practice. But as psychologist Kurt Lewin observed, there is nothing so practical as a good theory.[11] Dewey's passion for fighting against dualisms and "either/or" mentalities led him to write *Experience and Education* in 1938.[12] He recognized that some proponents of this philosophy deserted subject matter in favor of a student-centered, process approach to education. Dewey clearly valued *both* subject matter and educational process. The interaction of the two is the art of education, and engaging the continuity of human experience is central to the art of living.

### Education as Forming Moral Community

Dewey wrongly predicted in the early 1940s that the Progressive education movement would drop the term *progressive* and recast the debate into an argument over alternative views of the good of life.[13] To educate is to promote growth toward the good; to miseducate is to obstruct growth toward the good life. Unfortunately, the contemporary debate over the content, aims, and purposes of education most often is not cast in terms of understandings of the common good. Instead, one hears of educational reform oriented toward a recovery of the content of cultural tradition or a renewed emphasis in teaching basic skills, the "three R's." If our cities and culture are falling apart because of miseducation, then knowledge of the three R's will be of little value.

Democracy carries great weight in Dewey's conception of education.[14] He places great hope in the ability for a democratic system to promote the good of life. His hope, however, was not placed in the democratic institutions of his day. Rather, he viewed democracy as a way of being in the world. Dewey called for attention to the moral ideals of U.S. culture. An agnostic for much of his adult life, Dewey was hinting at a spirituality of education. Philosopher Richard Bernstein picks up on Dewey's spiritually charged conception of education and democracy by stating, "Democracy is a reflective faith in the capacity of all human beings for intelligent judgment, deliberation, and action if the proper conditions are furnished."[15] Even though he promoted the importance of moral ideals in culture, Dewey also was wary of moralism—the call for moral reform based upon a longing to recover the values of some golden era. As an alternative, Dewey placed his faith in the ability of education to provide models of community life oriented to moral living for U.S. culture. For Dewey, schools as social institutions and laboratories of moral living help shape the moral character of the culture.

Dewey became worried about the rise of industrialization in the United States and, more specifically, the dislocation of local communities.[16] In the first half of the twentieth century Dewey observed an emerging trend toward a type of corporate mentality that threatened to undermine local community life. The United States was beginning to become a mobile society, to view labor as a factor of production, and to emphasize profit as the "bottom line" in corporate culture. Dewey viewed schools as moral communities that might counteract the unsettlement of local communities. Moreover, Dewey called for a reconstruction and revitalization of local communities in search of the Great Community. His call, however, was not for a great uniform community; rather, he argued for a community of communities. Dewey's faith in schools might be put in this context because schools can provide a nexus for this dialogue among communities, especially in an increasingly mobile U.S. society.

Sometimes described as one of the primary promoters of secular humanism in the first half of the twentieth century, Dewey seemed to underestimate the potential of organized religion to accomplish the moral and aesthetic goals of human growth. He understood the organized religion of his time as being unwilling or incapable of promoting human growth as he conceived it. Fundamentalists, Evangelical conservatives, and Catholic conservatives accuse him of agnosticism and the denial of the power of religion. Yet Dewey's emphasis on community is consonant with most religious traditions. Moreover, his conception of growth as the aim of education can have transcendental religious implications that are consistent with Christian spirituality. Dewey's negative attitude toward religion seemed focused on its institutional dimensions rather than on the development of mature spirituality.

*Summary*

Four primary points emerge from this discussion on education. First, recognizing that many social institutions educate, we refer to the education of the public and not public education as traditionally conceived in schooling. Thus, the education of the public does not refer only to public tax-supported schools or to private and parochial schools, colleges, and universities. Individuals and the *paideia* are shaped by the ecology of social institutions that intentionally and systematically provide knowledge, skills, attitudes, values, and sensibilities. But family, mass media, politics, church, and other educative institutions often provide conflicting educational content and values, leaving individuals and communities fumbling for meaning in a fragmented, uncertain world.

Second, it is important to articulate the proximate and ultimate goals of education. Proximate aims of education indeed should be to teach subject matter, skills, sensibilities, and to inform the general public. Whether framed as education for global competitiveness or basic education, these proximate aims of education are important. At the same time, educational institutions also should consider their ultimate reasons for educating. Is education primarily for promoting the good of life, the common good? Is it primarily for enculturation into U.S. cultural tradition? Is it for individual freedom? Is it for emancipation? Answers to these questions enter the domain of values and ultimacy—the realm of spirituality.

Third, we need public conversation on education in order to make sense of the contemporary situation. This conversation needs to be disciplined and local in order to be effective. It is unlikely that anyone is educated into U.S. culture in general. Rather, we are educated into specific families, schools, and communities that interpret the culture. Someone educated in Los Angeles gets a very different message about life than someone educated in Juneau, Alaska, or Ames, Iowa. Perhaps the subject matter learned in schools is basically the same (although that is doubtful), but values, skills (street survival and environmental survival), and other sensibilities vary greatly. Thus, there is the need for communication among the various and sometimes radically diverse communities that make up U.S. culture. This conversation is our greatest challenge and our greatest hope for progressing as a nation with a pluralistic culture. Indeed, education is a problem. The more we appreciate its pervasiveness and diversity, the more likely it becomes that we can enter into informed conversation about it.

Fourth, public educators and Christian religious educators should have the same ultimate educational goal—growth. Public educators, more often than not, have labored under the assumption that education must be value-free or value-neutral. The truth is that all education is value-laden, if pursued to its ultimate ends. Dewey is correct in his contention that the aims of education should be growth. Christian religious educators should embrace this open-ended view of human potential as well. Theologians name it *transcendence*—a radical openness and movement toward that which is beyond ourselves.

Education has the power to expand horizons, to move beyond the confines of narrow thinking. Instead of pushing for prayer in public schools, churches could be more effective in promoting their own educational programs. Schools are not the only educational institutions in U.S. culture. Let the public schools engage in public education that acknowledges values, morality, and responsibility as part of holistic education. Specific perspectives on values, morality, and theology, however, should come from the churches.[17] But churches are not ready to meet this challenge. Too often Christian education means only Bible study from fairly narrow perspectives rather than an expansive understanding of education. But there is hope for another way of expressing and engaging in Christian religious education. The next chapter outlines how spiritual education can help Christian churches meet the challenge of the education of the public.

# Chapter 6 _____

# SPIRITUAL EDUCATION

George and Ellen raised three children and then separated. That seemed to be the story in a nutshell from George's point of view. After thirty-two years of marriage Ellen left a handwritten note for him in their half-empty house saying that they had drifted too far apart. Her attorney's name and telephone number were at the bottom of the note. The note said that she felt as if she had been living with a stranger for the past five years. George was mystified. He blamed their troubles on a Sunday School class Ellen attended. "Well, yes, it was five years ago she started attending that stupid class," he thought as he looked around the house in a daze. After the first year of her classes, Ellen started talking about a whole new world that was opening up to her. Time after time she invited him to attend with her, but he steadfastly refused. Ellen even begged him one Sunday to come to the next class. The only thing that George could imagine was "a bunch of women sitting around talking about the Bible and how Jesus loves them." Ellen said that it was not like that at all. And there were three men in their group of seven. But to George's way of thinking, it was just not a manly thing to do.

Ellen was tortured by her decision to leave. It was a desperate move. She hoped for a new life for her and George. But if it was to happen, it would have to come after this separation. Ellen was haunted by the scripture passage in Matthew's gospel that has Jesus saying, "For I have come to set a man against his father, a daughter against her mother . . . and one's enemies will be those of his household." She wondered what the Christian family values proponents had to say about that passage.

When Ellen told George she did not know him any more, she really meant that she had changed in her spiritual life. But George resisted all things spiritual. The Sunday School class was titled "Spirituality for Life." It was led by a retired pharmacist under the tutelage of the pastor. Ann, the pharmacist, had studied the Christian mystics throughout her life and wanted to pass on what she learned to others. The composition of the class changed from time to time, but basically the same group of people attended each Sunday. The pastor sat in on the class from time to time and noticed a change in the group's attitude about religion. Over the five years they had met, the class had moved from an attitude of wanting to find the "right" answers to religious questions to a search for a spiritual path to be followed in Christianity. The questions had become as important as the answers.

The class became a small community. One marriage had occurred, and Ellen was afraid that she and George would become the second divorce. She did not want that to happen, but that now was truly up to George. He would need to understand the search and growth in her spiritual life, and he would need to find his own way. She wished that he would search with her. It was a decision that he would have to make.

## SPIRITUAL EDUCATION DESCRIBED

George and Ellen's story is about education and spirituality. Although most people do not connect the two, the purpose of education, if pushed to its ultimate conclusion, is spiritual. This chapter addresses the difficulties of making this connection in a way that many Americans might agree with and understand.

We find ourselves a culture at risk and a church at risk. Despite advances in the sciences and the continuation of U.S. leadership in many world arenas, we have deep social ills. Secular humanists are wrong in placing hope for individual and cultural advancement solely in scientific and human progress. Fundamentalists are wrong in trying to inoculate culture with a particular brand of religious righteousness and a fire-and-brimstone cure. Can education address our problems? The answer is . . . maybe. If we conceive of education as primarily schooling in its current form, then the answer is clearly no. The answer is still no even if we view education in terms of the ecology of social institutions that educate. Even religious education as it is practiced in most Christian churches is not up to the task. There is hope to be found, however, in what we might call spiritual education.

The type of education needed for this contemporary, pluralistic, fragmented U.S. culture must be both comprehensive and useful. In this vein, spiritual education can be described as intentional meaning-making and value-laden learning that encompasses five interrelated realities: critical consciousness, authentic community, prophetic action, institutional identity, and spiritual growth. If any one of these elements is missing, learning is something other than spiritual education. To alter Dewey's purpose of education a bit, I propose that the ultimate purpose of education should be spiritual growth—not simply human growth. More proximate educational purposes vary according to many types of needs, but all education should have the potential of deepening people's spiritual life. This type of spirituality is not a passive, naive, other-worldly way of being. Rather, it engages the world with a passion for life and, at the same time, seeks deeper meaning and value. Spiritually educated people know the value of education. They recognize the usefulness of knowledge and skills and are able to contextualize them within a framework of ultimacy.

## Meaning-Making and Value-Laden Learning

The unpacking of this description of spiritual education begins with the idea of meaning and value as they relate to education. Reality is constituted through acts of meaning.[1] We soon leave the immediacy of the world of infancy to enter a world mediated by meaning, the world in which we live our lives. Meaning comes to us through human subjectivity, art, symbols, language, and the lives and deeds of persons.[2] In other words, we are constantly told, often in implicit ways, how to interpret life, how to make sense out of our experience. We come kicking and screaming into a sensory world that we try to understand. Infants read the faces, images, and sounds around them in an effort to make sense of their situation. The use of language expands that meaning-making world enormously. Art, symbols, and the significant people in our lives enlarge the meaning of our world and our place in it. We also make meaning through our dreams and intuitions. These creative interpretations of our situation bubble up from various levels of our consciousness in meaningful ways.

Education, in great part, introduces us to an expanded world of meanings as we become ever more familiar with cultural history, science, artistic expression, the professions, and even pop culture. We also are educated in how to interact with the natural world, our sense of place and space. The more varied and detailed these contexts and meanings are, the greater the fund of meanings with which we might interact. We are presented through education a world of meanings that give shape and context to our experience. This world of meanings forms what is commonly described as objective reality. The objective nature of this cultural reality, however, does not mean that it represents anything close to absolute truth. Rather, this is the reality, the world view, presented to us in our culture. Much of the educational enterprise, therefore, involves an individual's interaction with cultural, social, and scientific belief systems. We often are educated into conflicting belief systems, however, which heightens the need for us to refine our capability to choose between differing claims of truth and value.

Education should help us gain greater facility in understanding our process of decision-making and in analyzing the consequences of those decisions. As we are presented with the paradigms of cultural truth and morality, we make our own decisions and shape our own world view in relationship to the objective world view of the culture. These decisions may be quite different from what students articulate in the classroom. Students quickly learn what responses produce good grades and, all too frequently, that means a ready acceptance of the objective reality being presented by the educator. But over time, there emerges in us a personal world view, a set of decisions that form a basic belief system and stance toward life. Cultural objective world views become internalized and mediated into this personal world view. Growth occurs when we appropriate objective reality in such a way that it can be evaluated. This is the way of progress.[3] When, through education, we are able to recognize that our reality, our world view, comes from a particular set of cultural paradigms of truth and morality, cultural progress becomes more likely, and we become self-directed, empowered adults. In this conception of education, intentional meaning-making is constitutive of the educational process.

Human beings are natural meaning-makers. A primary task of education is to help us be as intentional as possible in our meaning-making. Much of the time we operate on automatic pilot; that is, we tend not to question the assumptions that form the basis for our understandings of what is true and worthwhile. Unexamined meaning-making is the result of unexamined assumptions and biases.

Value-free education does not exist, but some educators still persist in claiming that they exclude value perspectives from their teaching. In the first half of the twentieth century the myth of value-free education arose from scientific naiveté—the notion that once freed from the control of dogma and ideology, science could provide pure, unadulterated truth. The idea was that scientifically gathered data and logical analysis could "speak for itself." In value-free education, educators were free to teach the truth as they saw it and from the perspective of their disciplines. Sociologists and psychologists could theorize from cold, hard data with the same objectivity as natural scientists. The problem with this notion of education is that value choices must be made about what to study, what method to use, what data to gather, and what type of analysis to employ. Scientists and researchers know that value choices are made in the scientific process, and they know that the uses and consequences of their discoveries are value laden. The question is who controls the value choices.

Value-neutral education does not exist either. While very few educators now contend that education is value-free, the notion of value-neutral education seems to be alive and well. Value-neutral education asserts that good education consists of presenting all perspectives in the educational setting so that students can make up their own minds about the value of each perspective. It is difficult, however, to imagine how an educator can present all perspectives equally well. In an educational setting, value choices are made about what should be put into a curriculum, what should be left out, who is qualified to teach, and who is taught—all value-oriented questions and decisions. A completely value-neutral approach to education, therefore, is impossible. The way an educator chooses to teach is based upon a complex set of understandings and values about the human person and how a person learns.

## CRITICAL CONSCIOUSNESS

Another element of spiritual education is critical consciousness. I agree with philosopher-theologian Bernard Lonergan's contention that human knowing is a dynamic structure.[4] We come to knowledge in seemingly mysterious ways. Understanding, at times, seems automatic. At other times we cannot trust our initial understanding. We reflect on alternative understandings. For instance, if a person is an experienced driver, he or she immediately understands what to do when approaching a traffic light. If the traffic light is broken, however, the person does not have an immediate understanding of how to fix it. That understanding requires knowledge of electronics and municipal traffic light systems. Or if we read a passage from a book that we can connect with our existing knowledge, then it is fairly easy to understand. But if a passage is filled with terms that are unfamiliar, understanding becomes more difficult. We also might find ourselves faced with a dilemma that challenges our understanding of the right thing to do in a situation. For instance, if we believe that telling the truth is always a necessity, that belief can be challenged when an innocent life is at stake. We can see, then, that human knowing is much more complicated than developing a correct answer or making clear-cut choices. Knowledge and belief come from a dynamic process of being attentive to our experience of life, developing intelligent understandings, and making good judgments so that we can decide and act responsibly.[5]

Experiencing, understanding, judging, and deciding form different but interrelated aspects of human consciousness that enable us to come to knowledge and belief. As soon as we experience something through our senses or through our imagination or intuition, we feel the need to understand what we have experienced. Then there is the question of judgment. We judge the adequacy of our understanding according to our beliefs about what is correct or incorrect, good or bad. Based upon that judgment we decide on the adequacy of our judgment and what to do about it. This movement from experiencing to understanding to judging to deciding is part of the human constitution.

We constantly use this method to make the most ordinary decisions as well as the most complicated and painstaking ones. The difference lies in how intentionally and thoroughly we use it. Transcendence—radical questioning—forms the human dynamic that generates transcendental method. The way we come to knowledge and belief is transcendental because it is not confined to one particular field, discipline, theory, or to the realm of common sense. It compels us to know what is to be known and directs us to be attentive (to experience), to be intelligent (in our understandings), to be reasonable (in our judgments), and to be responsible (in our decisions).[6]

Human beings have an insatiable desire to know; almost every answer can be turned into another question. Transcendence opens new horizons beyond the world of immediacy—the world of individual knowing. Through our response to this transcendental ability we open ourselves to self-transcendence. We bring order out of chaos and make the unintelligible intelligible, over and over again. The human being is at once intelligent animal and transcendent spirit. To be attentive, intelligent, reasonable, and responsible is to be open to the fullness of consciousness, to the fullness of human potential and personhood. This description of human beings presents an image far beyond a conscious animal. We are creatures who have the potential to find meaning beyond ourselves—the realm of spirituality. This ability is part of what it means to be fully human.

### Our Assumptive World

According to Lonergan, these transcendental precepts (to be attentive, intelligent, reasonable, and responsible) provide a critical function for human beings. They enable us to be self-transcendent.[7] In other words, self-transcendence is a vehicle for living a spiritual life. Only when we attend to the data of sense and consciousness, apprehend the meanings that come to us, judge what is really independent of our formulations, and decide and act upon all that input are we exercising the best of our critical abilities. Thus, spirituality is not an other-worldly affair. It requires that we pay attention to the fullness of human consciousness.

All of the elements of human consciousness are interrelated. Critical method enables us to live responsible, spiritual lives. Our world of awareness is the world we live in; its size and complexity depend upon the amount of our lived experience and our awareness of it. Some might travel over the entire earth but remain relatively unaware of their experiences. Conversely, others may never travel far from their birthplace, yet their experiences may be quite broad through reading and imagination; their awareness of their experiences may be highly developed.

There also is sense of place in our world of awareness, a spatial quality. The place in which we live tends to shape our world. City dwellers have experiences vastly different things from those of people who live in rural areas. Likewise, people from different climates and cultures live in different worlds. Their different worlds of experience tend to shape their understandings, judgments, decisions, and actions. Really knowing other people, therefore, requires a good sense of their background and experiences. Really knowing ourselves requires an awareness of our own experiences.

Awareness of experience is not possible unless it includes understanding, judgment, and decision. The quality of our awareness depends upon how intelligently we understand our experience. Being intelligent, of course, is not necessarily the same as being educated. Formulating intelligent understandings in life comes from attentiveness to experience and depends upon good judgment and responsible decisions. Education gives us information and tools to create more expansive and critical understandings about our world.

Intelligence is the way we make sense out of life; it is our interpretive understanding of ourselves and everything around us. Intelligent people pay attention to their experience and make sense out of it in the best possible manner, given the tools they have to do so. Intelligent people know that their interpretations of experience are necessarily limited. Living intelligently means being open to other interpretations and willing to change our mind if other interpretations of experience make more sense; it also means defending our interpretation if other interpretations do not make sense. Intelligent people who become educated know the value of education and, at the same time, know the tentativeness with which judgments and decisions should be made.

Just as the quality of our awareness depends upon how intelligently we understand our experience, the quality of our intelligence depends upon our judgment. Being reasonable in our judgments means testing the veracity of our understandings with truth and value. The more highly developed our sense of truth and value is, the better the quality of our understandings—our interpretation of life. We receive our models of truth and value from our social and cultural situations.

A culture represents how models of truth and value become operative through the interaction of social systems. Models of truth and value for someone who primarily identifies himself or herself with a religious cult will be very different from those of an atheistic corporate executive. They both may live in the United States, but they live in very different worlds because their models of truth and value differ so greatly.

Reasonableness depends upon our notions of belief and knowledge. Belief and knowledge are intimately bound. Much of what we claim as knowledge in education is the socialization of the individual into a set of paradigms that are used to judge understandings and experience. Such is the social nature of knowledge. It is primarily through belief that knowledge is gained and passed on from generation to generation and from culture to culture. Being educated into a culture, as we all are through our families, schools, and the social ecology of educational institutions, means that we are enculturated into a set of belief systems. We use these belief systems to judge the reasonableness of our understandings and experiences. We trust in the belief systems of family, schools, religion, cities, and other social institutions. More specifically, we believe in the truth statements of mathematics, politics, literature, engineering, jurisprudence, and many other disciplines of learning. These belief systems carry their particular values with them. Being reasonable in our judging is often a matter of sorting through our belief systems.

Awareness, intelligence, and judgment make responsibility possible. Without awareness of experience, intelligence is purely speculative. Without judgment, intelligence is unsubstantiated. Without responsibility, judgment is untrustworthy. Put differently, responsible living requires judgment, intelligence, and awareness. Being critical means to attend to all of these aspects of consciousness in our decision-making. Conscious attention to this process is unnecessary for most of our everyday activity, but when it comes to important decisions or reflection on significant actions in our lives, paying attention to this very natural method is most important. Being responsible in life means reflecting on the assumptive world we have created for ourselves. This world consists of what we tend to pay attention to, the ways in which we interpret life, the assumptions that underlie our judgments, and the trustworthiness of our decisions and actions.

It would be dangerous and mistaken to view critical consciousness as a way of using dispassionate, logical precision on the messiness of life. Emotion and passion are part and parcel of the human constitution. Our emotions often direct what we pay attention to in everyday life. We can find clues to understanding in reflecting upon why our emotions are stirred. Good judgment is not dispassionate. We take emotion into account when we reason. Dispassionate decisions can be very dangerous. Weighty decisions tend to be emotion laden. Knowing the right thing to do in a situation is much different from actually doing it. Passion and emotion often move decisions into actions.

### Bias

The view of critical consciousness just described seems quite familiar to most people, though we seldom name the elements or even the process. But the flow from experience to knowledge and belief seems part of the human constitution. Why, then, do we not consciously use this method for all of our important decisions? The answer is bias. Lonergan contends that there are four types.[8] First, *dramatic bias* is the flight from the drama of everyday living to an inner world of fantasy. This bias is a refusal, intentional or not, to deal with insights that come from intelligence and common sense. Often it flows from an unwillingness to deal with the affective dimensions (our passions) of life as well. Consequently, we escape inward into our own assumptions and interpretations about life, unwilling to enter into a world of meanings outside of our self-created dreams, feelings, and vision of life.

Second, *individual bias* forms understandings and judgments based upon egoism. Undue attention to our own ego can result in an incomplete development of intelligence and responsibility. Unlike dramatic bias's flight from the drama of everyday living, egoism consciously looks to personal common sense and rationales to support our own view of life. Egoism scans the culture for our own benefit, intellectually and emotionally. Individual bias prevents an honest engagement with critical intelligence because of the danger of being wrong in our convictions. This bias is not naive. There is an occasional uneasiness that comes from a sense of being wrong or selfish. While ensnared in this bias, such pangs of guilt are quickly self-justified.

Third, there is *group bias*, which develops from unauthentic, unreflected-upon loyalty to our group and hostility to other groups—a form of group egoism. Group bias compels us to view the world from the perspective of what is good for the primary groups in our life. Whether the bond is family, profession, political party, or even race, the cohesion of like-mindedness can be seductive. There is the implicit tendency to shape our world view according to the views of the group. Group bias is a form of cultural blindness. It assumes that the common good is simply the composite of the assumptions and values of the cultural groups to which we belong.

Fourth, *general bias* is the composite shortsighted practicality of common sense. As Lonergan puts it, "To err is human, and common sense is very human."[9] Common sense often constitutes the expedient combined with the articulation of dominant group bias mixed with rather heavy doses of nonsense. Undoubtedly common sense does contain some collective knowledge and wisdom. Common sense, however, is not synonymous with collective wisdom. This criticism is not to deny the value of common sense as a way of negotiating the practical aspects of everyday human activity. Rather, to place common sense as a practical arbiter of right and wrong is to ignore its own biases.

### Conversions

The road to responsible living is indeed narrow, and dramatic bias, individual bias, group bias, and general bias often short-circuit the judging or testing process such that our understanding of truth and reality tends to be limited. Crises in our lives also may plunge us into a grasping for certainty that actually hampers awareness of experience, restricts understanding, limits judgments, and determines decisions. All of these obstacles to the unfolding process of the human spirit point to the need for conversion in human consciousness.

Lonergan claims that there are four types of conversion.[10] *Intellectual conversion*, simply put, breaks the myth that objectivity and reality are "out there" to be looked at and understood. The intellectually converted person understands that he or she lives in a world mediated by meaning and that knowing is not just experiencing the meaning contained in an objective world. Rather, knowing is experiencing, understanding, judging, and believing.

*Moral conversion* changes the reason for our decisions from satisfaction to values. We experience such a conversion when we realize that our choosing determines who we are and who we will become. The consequences of making choices based upon self-satisfaction as opposed to value become clearer. This does not mean the morally transformed person becomes morally perfected. It means that he or she tries to make moral decisions and actions in a world in which the truly good is far from being a matter of clear-cut choices. The morally transformed person struggles with the problem.

*Affective conversion* is a matter of both passion and commitment.[11] Knowing the morally right thing and doing it are two vastly different things. Affective conversion taps the enormous power of feelings to reorient radically the passionate desires of self-needs to a concern for the needs of others. We make a commitment to the ongoing struggle for acting based on the right thing to do. Affective conversion also can be viewed as a falling in love; that is, having feelings, passion, for the good of another person, groups of people, or an ideal. Whether it is being transformed by the love of another, a social cause, or a religious value, affective conversion gives passion and power to good intent.

Lonergan describes *religious conversion* as being grasped by ultimate concern and total self-surrender.[12] The religiously converted person chooses, decides, and acts out of unconditional love. The values of the common good change to ultimate value, to ultimate love. It follows that moral transformation is subsumed by religious conversion, thus forming an intimate connection. "Love of God and love of neighbor" is another way of putting it. If human beings are graced with God's love, then religious conversion is believing and acting upon such love. The "eye" of this love reveals this love in others and the values that extend from it—moral conversion. But are there connections with intellectual conversion?

Intellectual conversion pushes us to take seriously a world mediated by meaning. Realization of the tentative nature of the multitude of paradigms that we take for granted presses us, at some point, to take a stand in terms of values and beliefs in ultimates. It becomes easier to choose a philosophy or religious tradition as a way of evaluating reality—a way of making meaning in life. It is also easier to understand a chosen tradition as a story, a myth or paradigm that remains open for interpretation, enrichment, and revitalization. Intellectual conversion assists the process of becoming intellectually honest about religious belief.

### Historical Consciousness

An important element of critical consciousness is historical consciousness. Awareness of history is only part of historical consciousness. Being able to recall facts, events, dates, and key personages is not the central point. Knowing history includes understanding and judgment as well as data. Historical consciousness requires choosing among many alternative points of view. The authenticity of our choices depends upon the quality of the understanding and judgment we use to make our decisions. For instance, most adult Christians have not had the opportunity to learn about the history of Christianity, both its wonders and its warts. Consequently, Christian history is either ignored as irrelevant to faith or used selectively as historical proof-texting, that is, using a particular period or event to frame all of Christian history. For some Protestants the first few centuries of early Christianity and the Reformation comprise all of Christian history. Other Protestants view Christianity as a struggle against Catholicism. For some Catholics the Council of Trent (1545–63) or the Second Vatican Council (1962–65) is the primary historical referent. Other Catholics may understand the history of the papacy as the history of Christianity. Such historical perspectives are far from being authentic historical consciousness.

Historical consciousness demands that the intelligence, needs, and concerns of individuals and communities be put in constructive tension with the practicality of common sense. But common sense remains blind to its own inadequacies. In the long run, only a dialectic of history can adequately address oversights due to general bias.[13]

The movement of history can be characterized by two different cycles, a shorter cycle and a longer cycle.[14] The shorter cycle is composed the common sense of dominant groups in the culture. The longer cycle makes the questioning of common sense itself a possibility. Contemporary U.S. popular culture is ensnared in the shorter cycle, a composite of short-term common-sense approaches to social and cultural problems. In fact, cultural common sense even formulates the problems. Building more prisons is a short-cycle answer to crime and violence. The use of condoms is a short-cycle answer to teenage pregnancy. Most of our political answers to social problems are trapped in the shorter cycle.

Longer-cycle politicians are statesmen and stateswomen. Longer-cycle ministers are prophets. Longer-cycle people in U.S. culture are the visionaries who question our common sense. The long-range point of view understands the shortsightedness of change within the same mindset, myth, or ethos—variations of the same theme. This point of view reaches back into cultural tradition to recognize authentic development in order to put it in dialectical relationship with the concerns of the present so that authentic development may continue. The dialectic of history puts the knowledge, values, and aspirations of a community in tension with the movement of history. Given the perspective of history, what was considered the right and noble thing to do at one time in the community may not have been actually right and noble at all.

Historical consciousness exposes the group bias of the community and the general bias of common sense. And historical consciousness makes clearer the longer cycle of progress or decline in culture. Many of the solutions to community and cultural problems are dealt with in a short-term way, without historical perspective. The danger in this approach is that the alternatives available to solve problems become less and less comprehensive. Historical perspective, the longer cycle, makes accessible the more comprehensive viewpoint and, therefore, makes cultural breakthroughs possible.

### Authentic Community

Knowledge is not some individual possession.[15] Rather, it is a common fund from which we draw by our believing and to which we contribute by the authentic use of our critical conscious operations. Thus, community is more than a group of individuals who have common interests. Community occurs when common experience, understanding, and judgment lead to commonly held decisions that shape a way of life. Communities are dynamic and defy simple formulas for their creation. The attainment of common meaning may occur because of initial common interests or common practices or common ideals or even perceived common threats. Types of communities vary greatly. They may be ethnic, professional, familial, political, artistic, educational, and so forth. Progress in a community depends upon how well it passes on its knowledge, traditions, and practices, and how well community members critically apply, reshape, and revise this common fund of knowledge and beliefs in relation to the problems and potentials of the present and the future. Communities decline when they either lose common meaning in their decision-making or become disjointed from common experience, intelligent understandings, and reasonable judgments. The authenticity of community depends, therefore, on well-grounded decisions and actions.

Many adults participate in multiple communities. Culture is made up of various communities, and we tend to be educated in communities that interpret the culture. Education for authentic community recognizes this reality, plumbs the multiple meanings of the particular community, and explores with learners alternatives to this community-generated interpretation of culture and life. The authenticity of this aspect of education lies in the ability of the educator to present faithfully and genuinely the knowledge and aspirations of the community and to enable learners to engage the wider culture. The learner then receives an education in what it means to be a member of a particular community and also what it means to engage and respect other communities of interpretation. Miseducation teaches passivity and an inability to recognize irresponsibility in a community or in the interaction of communities.

## Prophetic Action

To prophesy is the public function of education. Lawrence Cremin explains, "Prophesy: in its root meaning, is the calling of a people, via criticism and affirmation, to their noblest traditions and aspirations. Prophesy, I would submit, is the essential public function of the educator in a democratic society."[16] This statement is quite striking, coming from a long-time historian of education and former president of Columbia University. His context and perspective is hardly that of religious education sectarianism. Education for prophetic action takes seriously the task of calling a community to its noblest traditions and aspirations. This prophetic task involves criticism as well as affirmation of community tradition—the promotion of authentic community. This prophetic identity also recognizes the value-laden and meaning-making roots of education.

Education for prophetic action is predisposed to action but not to unreflective activism. The difference lies in the degree to which action and reflection are connected. Reflective action utilizes the structures of human consciousness—the generalized empirical method—to decide upon proper courses of action. The starting point for this reflection may be attention to a problem in experience or the experience of action itself. In other words, it addresses both questions: Given this idea or experience, what should I do? and Given this action, how could I do it better? Reflective action keeps in tension theory and practice, action, and reflection.

This sort of predisposition toward action runs counter to many traditional ideas about education. The term *academic* has come to connote something or someone that is not practical. Education for prophetic action asserts that this notion of education needs to be countermanded. Kurt Lewin contends that there is nothing so practical as a good theory.[17] This saying might be applied to the educator in the sense that no one is more practical than a good academic.

Prophetic action requires a spirituality for the long haul. Prophets often raise the ire of people in power—and suffer the consequences. In order to call a community to its noblest aspirations and values, educators must act upon that calling themselves. Yes, we should talk about education as a calling. We remember the educators from our childhood and adolescence who not only possessed competence but had integrity as well. Educators do not only teach specific tasks or simply provide information; they offer insight on deeper dimensions of life and teach by the example of their lives. Prophets are despised as much as they are loved because of their steadfast dedication to excellence and justice. Being an educator means being attuned to the long search for meaning about the ultimate questions of life and helping others to be aware of that search in themselves.

## INSTITUTIONAL IDENTITY

Just as educators must know the community in which they educate, they also must know the institution in which they educate. If community emerges only from the attainment of common meaning, then, in order for an educational institution to be a learning community, there should be consensus on the meaning and aims of education. With this idea in mind, many educational institutions are far less than learning communities. More likely than not, Clark Kerr's long-time characterization of universities as *"multi*versities" still describes contemporary institutions of higher education.[18] Typically, instructors and departments teach according to the canons of their discipline. There are academic governance guidelines and administrative procedures to be attended to, but the overall thrust of educational concern is less toward educational issues and more toward publishing and research in each instructor's discipline. Thus, multiple affiliations and identities characterize universities, rather than a unified approach to education. Education with an awareness of institutional identity counters the "multiversity" notion of higher education, and presupposes that colleges and universities become educational communities.

Elementary and secondary schools have the same type of institutional problems. Often, administrative procedures mandated by local, state, and federal governments preoccupy school teachers and administrators. Educational philosophy and method seem to be luxury conversations. Classroom techniques and procedural issues of order and discipline take center stage. But when education becomes the centerpiece of conversation there is a greater chance for a school to become an effective learning community. Those schools that make education the center of their institutional life often succeed amid the culture of failure that surrounds them.

Similar educational concerns arise in other cultural institutions that educate. Corporations are now finding that attention to education at many different levels is integral to their success. The field of human resource development (HRD) is firmly established in corporate life in recognition of the importance of employee education and development. The continuous quality management process, the widely recognized new wave of business practice, also promotes education as a way of ensuring quality products and a dynamic organization. But unless businesses managers reflect on *why* they educate, including ultimate purposes, the quality of their institutional life suffers.

The idea of an educational community does not presuppose uniformity of opinion about education in the institution. In U.S. institutions of higher education, for example, the principle of academic freedom is a good and longstanding tradition. But the idea of an educational community does presuppose a dialogue among educators on the nature of the educational enterprise. Faculty, administration, staff, and students should be involved in this type of systematic reflection. The same might be said for elementary and secondary schools, corporations, and all institutions that educate in culture.

Institutional identity means that educators need to know not only how an institution educates its own members but how and why the institution educates the public. In other words, they need to know the institution's mission and place within society and culture. When this institutional identity is kept in mind, there is a benchmark to gauge the success and failures of educational efforts. If, for instance, a professional medical association's mission is to educate the public on the benefits of good health-care, then that mission should be adhered to in its educational efforts. If the association becomes fixated on the blind protection of its constituents' business interests, then the association's outreach efforts cease to be education. Promotion and advocacy would better characterize the information disseminated by the association. Distinctions among indoctrination, promotion, and training lead us to the final reality of spiritual education.

## SPIRITUAL GROWTH

Spiritual education takes seriously the ultimate implications of education. In fact, these implications are integral to the nature of education itself. They distinguish education from training and other short-term aims of teaching and learning. Philosopher Alfred North Whitehead claims that the essence of education is that it be religious. Notice that he does not claim that education *is* religious but that it should be religious. Education should instill a sense of duty and reverence in learners. As rational human beings it is our duty to learn as much as we can to make a positive contribution to society and to care for ourselves and our loved ones. Reverence comes from knowing that the present moment contains within itself the product of a not-forgotten past and the possibility of a future in the making. Eternity is the composite of all existence—present, past, and future. We have the ability to be right in the middle of it.[19] Whitehead challenges educators and learners alike to recognize the transcendent dimension of the moment and to take responsibility (duty) for creating the future. Education, according to Whitehead, should thrive on free inquiry and creativity as well as the human desire to know what is to be known with meaning and value integral to the educational endeavor. Whitehead's conception of the religious dimension of education is much different than sectarianism. He speaks of reverence and eternity. His description rings of spirituality.

### A Spirituality of Education

Parker Palmer, sociologist-educator and spiritual writer, rather surprisingly compares contemporary education with its historical taproot, monasticism.[20] Just as the monastery understands its mission as spiritual formation, Palmer asserts that contemporary education does something similar. He contends that the three monastic spiritual disciplines—the study of sacred texts, the practice of prayer and contemplation, and the gathered life of the community—are found in the public and private schools of our day. First, the sacred texts of secular school systems form their curriculum. These texts, of course, are not the sacred texts of the great world religions. But all one has to do is attend school-board hearings on the selection of textbooks to understand how sacred textbooks can be to a society. Children are being formed by the texts and curricula of their schooling. Fundamentalists fight for creationism; others fight for scientific theories of evolution. Minorities push for alternative perspectives on history because of the suppression of their achievements in traditional history texts. "History is written by the victors, not the victims," they claim. Others fight for a nonrevisionist approach to history, thereby preserving their understanding of cultural tradition. All sides of these educational battles realize the power of the books used in the education of their children. The same thing could be said for adult education. For good or bad, these academic disciplines have the potential to form "disciples" out of our children and ourselves.

Second, the spiritual disciplines of prayer and contemplation might seem far afield from what goes on in contemporary education. Nevertheless, there is a comparison. While there is no federally sanctioned policy allowing prayer in public schools, there are educational traditions analogous to monastic prayer and contemplation. Prayer and contemplation are spiritual disciplines that move us beyond and beneath the ordinary appearances of life; they propel us into the realm of ultimacy, the realm of truth. Much of twentieth-century U.S. education is devoted to the search for truth using the tools of reason and analysis. Parker Palmer contends that public education has used these academic tools as ways of searching for answers to the ultimate questions of life. The myth (doctrine) of objectivity has been a driving force in making reason and analysis keys to arriving at reliable truth. Just as the monks of old formed their students through habits of prayer and contemplation, contemporary educators form their students through the use of reason and analysis. Thus, fundamentalists and others who claim that public education is formation in a type of secular religiosity are somewhat correct. The reality of public education, however, is that its secular religiousness is not coherent or powerful because of fragmented curricula and debate over its aims. Nonetheless, Palmer is correct in including public education's search for ultimacy as a way of trying to satisfy the human desire for connection and wholeness—the realm of prayer and contemplation.

The gathered life of the community, Palmer's third comparison between monastery formation and contemporary education, is all too evident. Monasteries have been careful to structure their environment in ways that lend themselves to a consistent lifestyle. Communal life is an important part of the formation of young monks and the continued support of all monks. Similarly, the way schools and other educational institutions in society are organized teach just as powerfully as the content of any subject. For example, college courses on adult education are all but wasted if the college treats adult students like children with its administrative practices. Likewise, if church pastors preach about social justice but treat the church employees unjustly, their preaching falls upon deaf ears. If a corporation educates its employees about improved quality management but refuses to restructure itself to accommodate the changes necessary to improve, then the corporation will degenerate instead of improve.

Palmer's comparisons point to the spiritual dimension of education. Spiritual growth as the ultimate aim of education is an important corrective to Dewey's notion of human growth. But one could still ask, Spiritual growth toward what? The answer is twofold. First, we might answer in Deweyan fashion, "More spiritual growth," thereby acknowledging the openness of the human potential for spirituality. *Transcendence* is the term we normally give to such growth potential. Second, we might answer that our spiritual growth should be toward relationship with God and the rest of creation. Spiritual growth, then, forms a horizon for education that has connectedness—wholeness—as its ultimate aim.

Many educators might be troubled by such close connections between spirituality and education. They are concerned about spirituality being used as a vehicle for proselytizing others into a particular religion, or they may worry about the dominance of one religion over all others in a school's situation. Those concerns certainly are warranted because there is no such thing as a generic spirituality. Spirituality comes from a particular religious tradition. The world view that generally comes from Christianity predisposes Christians to that type of spirituality. There is an affinity for a personal relationship with Jesus Christ as a way of connecting with God, a dual devotion to communal worship and personal prayer, a commitment to righteous living generated by faith, and an accent on institutional stability. This type of spirituality tends to be very different from Jewish spirituality or Hindu spirituality or Native American spirituality or any other religious tradition. But spirituality is even more complicated. Spirituality also is unique to each individual. Everyone makes sense of his or her religious tradition or general attitudes toward God and other human beings according to his or her own experience and world view. No two Christians will have the same attitudes and interpretations about religion, God, and the world. Herein lies the mystery of spirituality; it depends upon an engagement with what ultimately can only be described as mystery. Our way of coping with mystery is through faith and trust. The challenge is to be as careful as possible about in whom or in what we place that trust; that care is a primary characteristic of mature spirituality.

Spiritual growth, then, is an ever expanding awareness of our own spirituality, its foundations (both personal and communal), and an ever increasing level of care that we take in placing our trust in the approaches and answers to the ultimate questions of life. Spiritual growth is a lifelong process and project. It is much more than answers to the ultimate questions of life. Spiritual growth is a way of describing the process that we use to answer those questions, and it describes the level of concern and carefulness that we use to evaluate the process and our answers. People who determine that there is nothing more to add to their own experience of spirituality or learning about the ultimate questions of life place themselves in a closed world that eventually will collapse under its own weight. In that world there is no room for critique, creativity, adventure, and, ultimately, there is no room for trust.

Even though agnostics and atheists are suspicious of religion, many of them have sympathy, if not a like affinity, for the ultimate questions of life. They may not claim spirituality as a term that is meaningful to them, but the concept of living a reflective life in the context of ultimacy has appeal to many nonreligious people. Their major concern is to avoid being coerced into a type of spiritual framework that has no meaning for them. A key insight to spiritual education is its emphasis on making a place for life's large questions in the educational enterprise. Thus, its accent is on methodology rather than answers. In other words, educators should help students raise spiritual questions but not give them definitive answers; assistance with answers should come from church and family, keeping in mind that spiritual questions tend not to have definitive answers. The foundational questions of life should be open to exploration.

In hindsight, the best educators I have encountered are those who engaged in spiritual education. Not only were they competent in their field, they also had the ability to excite their students with their enthusiasm and passion. These men and women had something else special about them. They had the ability to raise life's larger questions in the context of their field. I remember these wonderful educators not because of what they taught but because of who they were and the context into which they placed the education. It always was the larger context of life. They were people in love with their field and passionate about life.

When educators attend to critical consciousness, authentic community, prophetic action, institutional identity, and spiritual growth, they better ensure meaning-making, value-laden learning. These educational realities constitute an ideal environment for education. Most educational settings, however, are far less than ideal. The tendency is to place emphasis on only one or two of these realities. Public schools, for instance, tend to accentuate critical consciousness and institutional identity at the expense of prophetic action and spiritual growth. Many parochial schools, on the other hand, stress authentic community and spiritual growth to the detriment of critical consciousness and prophetic action. These dualistic, fragmented views of education ill equip schools for the challenges of contemporary U.S. culture. The Catholic school system, for example, was built by immigrant Catholic communities over the past century to protect Catholic identity in a primarily Protestant U.S. culture. Catholic parents were taught that it was their duty as parents to educate their children in Catholic schools. Thousands of religious sisters and brothers staffed the schools, and most parishes in cities with a significant Catholic population had Catholic schools. Thus, authentic community and a form of spiritual growth were primary identifiers of Catholic schools. The origin of U.S. Catholic parochial schooling mirrored the social situation of Catholic communities. But as Catholic schools began to expand their mission from religious enculturation to include academic excellence and good citizenship, Catholics also began to succeed in U.S. culture, so much so that a Catholic became president in 1960. The election of John F. Kennedy, for most Catholics, signified cultural success.

Catholic schooling was a vehicle for the Catholic community's coming of age. But that success had a price. The Catholic schools of the 1990s, unlike the Catholic schools of a century ago, are searching for their Catholic identity. It is not unusual for contemporary Catholic schools to have non-Catholics make up a large percentage of their student and faculty populations. Catholic schools are now known more for their emphasis on Christian values, discipline, and academics than for their role in enculturation. Catholic schools now also serve a more affluent student population than they did in their early years. In most cases this shift has been unavoidable because of the need to compensate adequately lay teachers and administrators. The sisters and brothers who supported the Catholic schools with their labor and dedication in the first part of this century are now gone. That type of service cannot be duplicated by lay educators who have families to support. The revitalization of contemporary U.S. Catholic schools depends upon their integration of the four dimensions of spiritual education.

## SPIRITUAL EDUCATION REVISITED—A SUMMARY

We have seen that in the beginning formal education in the United States had an explicitly religious agenda. The Christian Bible was used as a primary text well into the twentieth century. Some educational critics contend that secular humanism, with its atheistic modernist agenda, has replaced Christianity as a religious and moral rudder for students from pre-kindergarten through college. Christianity is no longer the moral glue keeping schools accountable for academic and character formation. The same educational ecology of family, church, schooling, and work place no longer support one another in the education of the moral Christian citizen. The United States truly has entered a pluralistic era with a recognition of the damaging effects of placing one religion as the unofficial standard for state-supported education. Americans of other faiths point out, however, that Christian values are explicitly proclaimed in Congress, local school boards, and corporations. Political campaigns still proclaim that this country was founded upon Christian (not Deist) principles, and it is those principles that made this country great. The Christian majority wants to be tolerant, for the most part, but has yet to learn how.

Not only are schools in trouble today, but so are other social institutions—family, church, mass media, politics, the legal system, and corporations. We the People have placed our hope for a better life in education. We assume that if only we can fix the schools, all will be well. But schools cannot bear the burden of fixing all of society's ills.

Schools work well only when there is support from family, church, and the other educational institutions in society.

A way out of this social and cultural quandary is through spiritual education, and it is the churches that must lead the way. Churches can, and indeed must, explicitly draw upon their religious tradition to educate for coherent moral, intellectual, affective, and religious transformations. In this way churches can support family life as well as quality public schools, ethical politics, just legal systems, and scrupulous commerce. Spiritual education as intentional meaning-making and value-laden learning can best occur in churches. If there is the will do so, churches can support the five interrelated realities that form spiritual education: critical consciousness, authentic community, prophetic action, institutional identity, and spiritual growth.

# Chapter 7 _____

# SPIRITUAL HIGHER EDUCATION

Jim sat transfixed by what he was hearing. For the first time he was encountering an explanation of theology that made sense to him. The bespectacled, forty-ish Jesuit theologian who taught the class brought very dense theology alive. The class was made up of Catholic sisters and lay people who were pursuing the master's degree in religious education. Jim, ostensibly, was there for the same reason, but he was searching for a theology that made sense to him. At age thirty he was seeking a more complete explanation of his Catholic faith. The churches he attended, Catholic and otherwise, did not meet his needs. He suspected that his intellectual bent got in the way of his faith, but he felt the need to be intellectually honest about what he believed. For quite some time the religion of his childhood had been breaking apart, and there was no process for putting it back together as an adult. He hoped this class would help.

The Jesuit lectured about the need for theology to start with an understanding of who human beings are rather than starting with who God is; most theologians start with the concept of God. His lectures were animated.

> If we first find common ground in our humanity, then it is more likely that we can talk about our concept of God. The Bible presents earthy reflections about God. But we have not learned from the Bible. Instead, we tend to start theological speculation about God with theoretical doctrines and not from our experience as human beings. Theology has tended to leave "us" behind and, thereby, keeps itself in the theological stratosphere, and that gives the impression that God is above the concerns of everyday life. That message is the opposite of what the Bible

tells us about Jesus. He talks about God as being with us in life's struggles, like a father waiting for his wayward son. The theological task of our time is to integrate in a faithful and credible way the earthy theology of the scriptures with the intellectual theological traditions of the past two millennia.

Jim could not contain himself. He blurted out, "Why have I been lied to all my life? I have heard from the pulpit only simplistic stories about Jesus and a naive explanation of theology and life. When I ask priests and preachers whom I consider to be friends about this, they say that most people do not have the education to understand a sophisticated interpretation of scripture and theology. They say it only confuses most adults. So, am I to believe that the truth is only for the theologically educated? There has to be a better way." Jim looked around as he finished. The rest of the students were frozen in place. The Jesuit had a big smile on his face. He said, "You are here to find a better way."

Ralph's life was dedicated to astrophysics. A gifted teacher and researcher, he was a rising star in academia. His problem was that he was a mystic. Ralph's fascination with astronomy and physics went far beyond mathematics and the study of natural forces. The deeper he went into his research, the more he was convinced about the sacredness of the universe. This type of talk, however, did not sit well with his fellow researchers. He turned off the atheists in his department and alienated other colleagues who had traditional religious views. Only Theresa, who had no formal religious affiliation, could identify with Ralph's spirituality.

Ralph saw no difference between the aims of pure research and the ethical implications of how that research is used. He even went deeper than ethics and dared to talk about spirituality. Other members of the department thought that their sole task was to teach physics. Ethics and morality should be left to philosophers and theologians. But Ralph thought it was his responsibility as a physicist to make those connections in his classroom. Not that he required his students to agree with his opinions, but he wanted ethical and spiritual questions raised. At first his students were amazed and a bit uncomfortable about such questions. Their first response always was, "Will this be on the test?" He would quickly respond, "These issues are life questions, not test questions." Once that was cleared up, his students became content with his occasional spiritually oriented probes. To Ralph's amazement and delight, a group of physics graduate students approached him about forming a discussion group on the spirituality of the physicist. As quickly as Ralph said yes, his department chairman said no. He protested to the university president, but to no avail. Ralph left academia never to return. His research continues in a privately funded laboratory, and he writes and speaks in nonacademic settings.

## HIGHER EDUCATION AND SPIRITUALITY

Findings from a 1982 study indicate that on sixteen measures of religiosity ranging from frequency of church attendance to a sense of spiritual commitment, virtually all measures indicate a negative relationship between educational level and religiosity.[1] Research studies differ in their findings according to variables such as the orientation of the educational institution (church-related or secular), the intellectual orientation of students (understanding science and religion as antithetical or understanding science and religion as compatible), the degree of religious commitment of students entering the institutions, and the particularities of religious denominations, but the higher education in general adversely affects the religiosity of its students.

More recent findings suggest the same inverse relationship. In a 1991 poll, 63 percent of high school graduates who did not go to college agreed with the statement that religion can answer all or most of today's problems; only 53 percent of respondents with a college degree agreed. In the same poll 33 percent of high school graduates and 42 percent of non-high school graduates indicated a great deal of confidence in organized religion, while only 26 percent of college graduates expressed a great deal of confidence.[2] What accounts for this inverse relationship? One answer is that higher education incorporates many different philosophies about life into its programs of study, some of which are openly antagonistic to religion. A 1992 report found that even though approximately 55 percent of U.S. residents say that religion is "very important" in their everyday lives, almost no one says that religion should be "very important" in higher education.[3] Despite rather stable religious beliefs in the general population over the past five decades, the consensus is that higher education has become increasingly secularized.

### Religion and Higher Education in the United States

Ironically, contemporary secular U.S. higher education has its origins in the denominational colleges of the eighteenth century.

Harvard, Yale, William and Mary, and Georgetown, among many other universities, had sectarian beginnings. Their purpose was to provide an educated clergy for the colonies and to serve the educational needs of the local community. Separation of church and state in higher education did not become an important issue until the twentieth century. It was presumed in the eighteenth and nineteenth centuries that Protestant religious values were the glue that held society together and that those values would permeate education at all levels. Reading the Bible in the classroom was not a problem. Religious freedom meant that other religious groups had the right to construct their own schools and colleges with alternative religious perspectives. The most successful example has been the massive educational system built by U.S. Catholics. Until the twentieth century, separation of church and state did not mean a separation of religious values from education. The consensus has been clear that the United States is a Christian nation. While this contention has been challenged over recent decades, there has been a recent resurgence of concern about the need for common religious and moral values.

Americans place a lot of faith in education. Douglas Sloan argues that just as a chief role of the established church in medieval Europe was to provide common social values for society, the role of education in nineteenth-century America was to do the same.[4] The promotion of common social values as the glue of societal harmony thus moved from the realm of coercion associated with the established church of European countries to the realm of persuasion associated with U.S. educational institutions. Americans believe in the persuasive power of education to build social unity and national community. Jefferson called for an educated, enlightened citizenry as a necessity for a democratic republic. Education also has been viewed as the balance wheel of national social machinery and as an embryonic community to form thoughtful citizens. Americans have placed their trust and belief in a combination of education, values, and social harmony in their great search for national identity. Schools and colleges have been positioned as the social vehicles for the enculturation of U.S. citizens and, just as important, for the assimilation of immigrants into this identity.

Most eighteenth- and nineteenth-century colleges had very small student populations, but there were many colleges throughout the country. They have had a big influence on U.S. culture. Nineteenth-century small denominational colleges helped shape national identity in three ways. First, they consciously promoted common social values that partly gave rise to U.S. civil religion. We talk matter-of-factly about the dignity of the individual and inalienable human rights. These notions have a religious base and, in great part, have become part of U.S. cultural common sense through education.

Second, the college president usually taught a senior moral philosophy course aimed at helping students integrate curriculum learnings and providing a means for the ethical application of knowledge. The president was typically a member of the clergy or a deeply committed Christian.

Third, college graduates were expected to make a difference in society. As learned people, graduates were to use the intellectual unity gained in their study of literature, the arts, and science to exercise an enlightening and unifying influence on the wider society. Thus, nineteenth-century denominational colleges operated under the assumption that higher education constituted a single unified culture. This educational approach considered literature, the arts, and science equal parts of a whole. This approach also challenged graduates to synthesize and integrate this single unified culture into a beneficial personal stance toward life and society.

The rise of the modern university in the late nineteenth century challenged the unified culture of small denominational colleges. Modern U.S. universities arose at a time of social fragmentation and a change in the conception of the relationship between knowledge and society. Urbanization and social problems resulting from new ways of viewing work and society began to tear at the existing fabric of U.S. society. But this change did not occur overnight. Large Midwestern public research institutions such as the universities of Michigan, Wisconsin, Indiana, and Illinois had clergy presidents and predominantly clergy faculty as late as the mid-to-late 1800s. It was not unusual to require daily chapel attendance and such courses as "Evidences of Christianity" and "Natural Theology." Secularization, by some accounts, occurred through the movement of a conservative Evangelical form of Protestantism to liberal Protestantism.[5] Christianity, whether conservative or liberal, still was presumed to be the religious and moral fabric of the culture. But as the nation entered the twentieth century, the liberal arts nature of the curriculum changed. At the same time, the rise of popular education at all levels, with higher education at the pinnacle, gave educational access to a wider range of societal groups. This increased access to higher education also brought with it an increased respect for technology and the role of the specialized expert in society.

The nineteenth-century college's unified culture of learning also began to fragment and split into separate branches. Most significantly, science emerged as the dominant paradigm for authentic learning and knowledge—so much so that fields of study oriented more toward subjective meaning and value (art, literature, music, religion) began to pale in comparison to the apparent objectivity and certainty found in science. Science came to be aligned with the objective, the technological, the productive, the true. Conversely, religion, the arts, and the humanities became associated with the subjective, the ideological, and the arbitrary. While Christianity was still the predominant religious cultural influence in the first half of the twentieth century, religion has lost respect in higher education. Once the Queen of the Sciences, theology has been relegated to either sectarian religious ideology or to the academic study of religion as a cultural phenomenon. Religion has moved from a central place in the higher education of the nineteenth century to an educational aside in the twentieth century.

### An Orthodox Theory of Knowledge

Contemporary higher education now finds itself in conflict. Universities continue to recognize the importance of promoting meaning, value, and common social purpose. Yet, a narrowed view of truth and conception of knowledge discount those very subjects (religion, arts, and humanities) that deal most specifically with meaning and value. Higher education is in need of a radically different theory of knowledge that recovers an equal balance among science, religion, and the rest of the liberal arts in order to correct the overemphasis placed on science and technology. This radicalism is not a return to nineteenth-century notions of the role of Christianity in culture. It involves a different way of viewing knowledge and belief.

Before outlining such a radical theory of knowledge, it is necessary to understand the orthodox epistemology that has pervaded higher education. Sloan describes this epistemological orthodoxy as having adopted a narrowly quantitative, materialistic, and functionalist view of knowledge with such zeal that it tends to exclude feeling, imagination, the will, and intuitive insight from the domain of rationality—or to accord them only the most limited importance— and to deny any place for mind, meaning, and persons as constituent of reality.[6] This orthodox view of knowledge minimizes the qualitative dimensions of experience to such an extent that it almost reduces the qualitative to subjective nonsense. It promotes the idea that we know only what we can measure and use. Sloan describes this understanding of knowledge as a "scientistic" and "technicist" world view.

Sloan does not argue with science per se. Rather, he critiques the view of science that has become orthodox, that is, science with positivistic foundations. Through the heritage of scientific materialism, scientific naturalism, and logical positivism, this orthodoxy makes assumptions about knowing, the human being, and the world. Namely, science provides our only sure way of (a) knowing the world; (b) knowing the place of human beings in the world; and (c) knowing, with some degree of certainty, the total picture of the world. While even this narrow scientific view and its accompanying technology have provided many advances at all levels of human activity in the twentieth century, they also have provided deadly tools of war as well as the potential of worldwide ecological disaster. In higher education this epistemological orthodoxy reflects reductionism and functionalism in the social sciences. This orthodoxy appears in schools of education as behaviorist and mechanistic models of human development and learning.

As the inadequacies and consequences of scientism and technicism become more and more evident, educational institutions have tried to seek correctives. Increasing interest in moral education, values clarification, liberal arts general education, the teaching of ethics in professional education, and various new specializations in ecological studies all have appeared over the past few decades. The problem with such programs is that they understand values as directing the *application* of knowledge. They do not understand values as *constitutive* of knowledge—as assumptions that, in fact, determine what is true and correct. The limited effectiveness of these educational initiatives seems due to the fragmentation this epistemological orthodoxy fosters. In short, Sloan argues that this epistemological view cannot deal with "(1) normative and intrinsic values—science [scientism] can deal only with descriptive and instrumental values; (2) purposes—the question of "Why?"; (3) global and existential meanings—ultimate questions and the problems of life; and above all, (4) qualities—qualities that involve feeling, awareness, and life."[7] The corrective to this orthodox scientistic and technicist world view, which intentionally disconnects knowledge and values, is found in a radical reshaping of our understanding of what constitutes knowing.

### A Radical Theory of Knowledge

If higher education is to recover a holistic approach to learning, it can do so only with an epistemological radicalism that transforms our ways of thinking and knowing to consider meaning, qualities, and the value of persons as integral to knowledge and reality. The values, needs, and intentions of the learner shape learning. This view transforms a conception of knowledge as learning objective facts and their ethical application to a more holistic view of knowledge that acknowledges feelings, imagination, and values as constitutive of knowledge. Sloan argues that the beginnings of such a transformation are found in a radically different conception of knowledge. He terms this radical epistemology "insight-imagination," describing it as "the involvement of the whole person—thinking, feeling, willing, valuing—in knowing."[8]

Robert Bellah expresses similar concerns about contemporary higher education. He contends that cognitive rationality forms the central value that organizes modern university education. But the fullness of cognitive rationality tends to be minimalized. "It [cognitive rationality] is simply a means. Knowledge is a tool for the manipulation of the world. The pervasive emphasis on the manipulative, instrumental use of knowledge has tended to make of the university a kind of universal filling station where students tank up on knowledge they will 'need' later."[9] Bellah calls for a recovery of the richness of cognitive rationality that includes a holistic notion of disciplined knowing. In this conception, cognitive rationality means much more than acquiring knowledge. It also means learning to learn, self-awareness, and includes an openness to transcending the rational and merging with nonrational ways of knowing. Bellah concludes that a new religious consciousness must transform higher education. This consciousness understands criticism as valuable, yet limited. Rational critique cannot explain everything. In fact, rational critique at its heart is a form of interpretation, and no interpretation of reality comprises the totality of reality. This new religious consciousness calls for higher education to promote an appreciation of religious symbols and traditions that offer different interpretations of reality.

Americans have placed their faith in higher education to promote common values and social harmony. Because of a tendency to emphasize a value-free approach to science and knowledge, fragmentation in a unified culture of learning, and a corresponding deemphasis on meaning and value found in the arts and humanities, it appears that higher education has moved from a holistic approach to a conflictive approach to education.

How might colleges and universities recover religious dimensions of the educational enterprise and create an approach to education that accommodates value and religious meaning? This question has been more of a concern for church-related higher education than for private and state higher education. There are a number of ways in which denominational colleges and universities have attempted to recover the religious dimensions of education. Are there lessons to be learned from them for U.S. higher education in general? As with most complex questions, the answer is in part yes and in part no.

## CHURCH-RELATED HIGHER EDUCATION

Church-related higher education institutions have access to a unifying element for the total college experience, namely, their faith tradition. But the reality often is quite different. Doctrinal disputes and ecclesial struggles in church-related colleges have a tendency to add another layer of fragmentation on top of an already fragmented curriculum. In many ways, church-related colleges are searching for ways of integrating spirituality into their institutional life. The only difference between them and most secular institutions is the search. Denominational colleges and universities are concerned about the spiritual life of their students. Administrators and faculty, however, are divided as to how to approach the problem.

### A Departmental Strategy

An obvious way of addressing the spiritual dimension of higher education is through a college department of religion. A study of departments of religion in fourteen church-related American colleges and universities outlines a general progression of identities—from confessional particularity to ecumenical theism to religious pluralism.[10] This progression reflects a movement from a Christian studies orientation with courses on biblical history and interpretation to more pluralistic offerings with courses on Asian religions and peace studies. Viewed differently, this progression of departmental identity describes an evolution from traditional systematic theology to the history of religions, to the emergence of new theology, to religious studies. Typically these trends are the result of influences from professional communities, sponsoring religious bodies, the educational institution, students, and faculty outside the department. While the movement toward a more inclusive sense of religiousness seems clear enough, the role of the department seems unclear beyond the responsibility of educating majors in the field. Moreover, one might ask if is it prudent to charge one department with the task

of providing a much needed spiritual dimension to the higher education curricula—as if by inoculation.

### An Interdisciplinary Strategy

Another strategy takes a more interdisciplinary tack.[11] Proponents
of this approach lament about higher education's specialization and
compartmentalization, especially in the isolation of religious studies courses from other academic disciplines. Efforts are made to
integrate religious tradition with humanities teaching. Courses in
Christian humanism serve as an interdisciplinary meeting ground
for the religious and secular dimensions of education. This approach
advocates that Christianity and the humanities be correlated in such
a way that students do not have to choose between Christ and culture; instead, students might integrate the insights of Christian humanism in the context of contemporary living. Interdisciplinary
Christian humanism courses, then, serve as integrating points in
the college curriculum—an expanded and updated idea, perhaps,
of the nineteenth-century denominational college senior moral philosophy course.

### A Campus Ministry Strategy

Campus ministry programs on denominational and secular higher
education campuses long have sought to meet the religious needs
of their student and faculty constituencies. Comprehensive campus
ministry programs are ecumenically sensitive and incorporate a
scholar or theologian-in-residence position on their staffs. Moreover,
vibrant campus ministry programs initiate dialogue among disciplines over contemporary moral and ethical issues as well as coor-
dinate social outreach programs. A problem arises when campus
ministries are depended upon, in much the same fashion as a department of religion, to provide a tangential religious element to
education, focusing on only those students who feel inclined to participate voluntarily.

### An Institutional Strategy

Some church-related colleges view themselves in a clearly denominational way. They adhere to church orthodoxy as outlined by church
leaders and require strict observance by both students and faculty.
One example is the Great Books type curriculum of a small Catholic
college that claims to foster a profound sense of religiousness in
students.[12] Throughout all four years students study theology, philosophy, mathematics, grammar, and experimental science. Moreover,

faculty make a conscious attempt to help students integrate their learnings through weekly seminars. Methodological in focus, these sessions aim at helping students identify and articulate connections among subjects. The curriculum places theology and adherence to Roman Catholic Church teachings as foundational to the educational enterprise and uses such adherence as a referent for the integration of student learnings. Thus, the institution identifies its goals and purposes as theological (in this case aligned with a conservative Catholic position) and uses a traditional liberal arts curriculum. Students entering this institution clearly are presented with its distinctive liberal arts approach to education and its conservative Catholic approach to religion. In a sense, the college organizes its curriculum according to compatible educational and religious positions. While this institutional approach addresses the need for integrating a religious world view and an educational philosophy, one might question the appropriateness of such a dogmatic institutional strategy for a pluralistic culture.

These various programs and strategies of denominational colleges and universities all, in their own way, promote the value of religion in higher education. They stop short, however, of articulating an epistemological radicalism that is needed in contemporary higher education. The institutional strategy is closest to articulating a comprehensive approach to education, but it does not articulate an educational philosophy that accommodates religious values with the values of free and pluralistic inquiry.

We have, then, a situation in which higher education in the United States over the past two centuries has moved from its denominational college origins with a unified culture of learning situated in a primarily Protestant religious ethos to a primarily secular institution that espouses a value-free, objective approach to education and is situated in pluralistic ethos. The history of Catholic higher education over this same time period has had a similar story line, but there also have been major differences.

### AMERICAN CATHOLIC HIGHER EDUCATION—FINDING CATHOLIC IDENTITY

Prior to Power's 1958 study, there were very few, if any, comprehensive histories of Catholic higher education in the United States.[13] Catholic higher education histories tended to be dissertations devoted to the history of a particular college or to a specific period in U.S. history. Power's work places the development of Catholic higher education in the context of the changing American social scene.

Phillip Gleason employs the same contextual approach and fine-tunes his analysis by identifying three areas that distinguish Catholic higher education's heritage from U.S. higher education in general.[14] First, socially, students and faculty were different from other American teachers and students. Aside from a relatively few French and Spanish, Catholics in the United States were latecomers as immigrants to the "promised land." Along with the handicap of being foreigners in a new country, these immigrants in the nineteenth century felt strongly the vestiges of the eighteenth-century U.S. "papist" suspicion of Catholics, which lasted well into the twentieth century.

Second, institutionally, the patterns of educational organization and administration were different. Clerical control of administrations, primarily by religious orders, diverged significantly from U.S. norms. The rather strange-sounding 1835 Georgetown University seven-year A.B. Jesuit curriculum based upon the *Ratio* is an example. Accommodations to the standard U.S. four-year curriculum were soon made, although some seminaries in the United States still vary from this format.

Third, ideologically, the ideas, beliefs, and attitudes of Catholics tended to be very different from many other U.S. educators. The transition of U.S. higher education from a liberal arts college to the research university placed Catholic higher education in a quandary. The emerging disciplines (psychology, sociology, and specialized disciplines of the physical sciences) appeared in the curriculum. The introduction of the credit-hour system, an elective curriculum, the standardization movement, and interventions by accrediting agencies complicated matters even further. Allied with other critics of the quantification and bureaucratization of higher education, Catholic faculty and administrators objected to the emergence of vocationalism, the depersonalization of the academically neuter credit-hour unit, and the generally fragmented confusion of U.S. higher education. The basis of their critique, however, distinguished Catholic educators from other critics. Gleason argues that for the Catholic critics "these weaknesses were but a faithful reflection of the chaos and confusion of the modern mind, which had lost its anchorage in religious and philosophical truth. Their own approach, Catholics believed, effected a synthesis of classical humanism, sound philosophy, and true religion."[15] These criticisms were not unique to Catholic educators. But coupled with the two other areas of difference, this judgment set Catholic higher education further apart from the mainstream.

Despite these differences, Catholic higher education set about preparing students for entry into society. The only means of entering into society was to find ways of accommodating to the U.S. scene. Thus, the story of Catholic higher education in the United States is one of a constant flow of separation from and accommodation to U.S. culture. Utilizing Niebuhr's models of Christ-culture relationships, Robert O'Gorman traces the movement of Catholic education in the United States according to this flow and identifies three eras:

> (1) [church] *against culture*—the "siege" mentality (1790–1920): "God's people" are under attack and a "fortress" is built to keep Catholics separated from U.S. culture; (2) [church] *above culture*—the "Catholic civil faith" mentality (1920–1960): "God's people" call for the conversion of the rest of the nation to become the City of God and build a "ladder" up which U.S. culture is beckoned to climb to a Catholic Christendom; and, (3) [church] *in the culture*—the "pluralist" mentality (1960–the present): Catholics present in the midst of the populace as "yeast" by which they permeate, serve, and prophesy to the culture.[16]

The differing theological visions of these eras indicate very different versions of Catholic self-understanding, which in turn gives direction to Catholic education. The preservation of religious identity for U.S. Catholicism in what O'Gorman describes as the first two periods was particularly strong. A community under siege tends to "circle the wagons" and raise its children within the circle.

In the second era, a community that perceives itself as having a mission to convert the rest of culture wants to ensure that its children know who they are and whom they need to convert. The "ghetto" parish with a school in its enclave seemed the most appropriate response in the first period for protecting the inherited religious identity that came to this country. The Catholic school in the second period, however, moved from being protected in the parish enclave to being a means of integrating into the wider society. The school, in a sense, became the ladder for the way up socially and spiritually.

The third period (1960–the present) presents a very different educational challenge. Contemporary Catholics are a majority Christian denomination in the United States, with a membership that includes some of the most influential people in this country. On the separation-accommodation pendulum, U.S. Catholicism now struggles to swing from the accommodation characteristic of the second era toward a separation from culture in the third era. The distinctiveness of Catholic identity in U.S. culture can no longer be presumed; it

needs to be discovered. In many respects the ghetto of Catholic identity is gone. Many Catholic schools (including colleges and universities) are disappearing along with the ghettos. Most Catholics now
live, worship, and are educated in a truly pluralistic U.S. culture. A
primary task for Catholic education, in this view, is to find ways of
forming its students and transmitting a way of life that respects both
Catholic tradition and a pluralistic U.S. culture. This educational task
is difficult, if not impossible, for Catholic schools because these
schools are no longer supported by a uniform Catholic ethos—family, ghetto community, church. As O'Gorman suggests, U.S. Catholicism might look beyond schooling to more of a socialization model
of education that utilizes basic ecclesial communities, both within
and without parish structures, as well as other vehicles for the formation of Catholic identity.

### A Catholic Philosophy of Education

Catholic higher education in this pluralistic era faces questions of
identity and purpose. In the late 1960s Catholic higher education
entered a significant period of change. Students and faculty in Catholic
colleges and universities began to question what made their institutions religiously distinctive. Catholic higher education in this period
began asking what the connection between church and university
should look like. Hassenger makes two rather significant points about
Catholic higher education in that period.[17] First, he argues that the
U.S. Catholic university needs to be distinguished from the magisterial teaching authority of the church. In so stating, he understands
Catholic colleges as being a part of the Catholic church in a more
personal sense than institutional sense. Catholic higher education
should be concerned with educating individuals oriented to the world
from the perspective of a religious tradition. Catholic colleges should
not be places of arbitration and official pronouncement of church
doctrine; rather, they should be places in which Catholic tradition is
explored and investigated. Second, the environment of the Catholic
college should promote the personal development of the individual.
Hassenger understands this development as intellectual, moral, and
religious. Thus, he contends that Catholic higher education should
foster "an atmosphere where ultimate questions are asked and a
diversity of standpoints presented."[18] This approach to education
certainly seems appropriate for the contemporary situation, but it
also presents a very difficult challenge to Catholic higher education.
    John Elias indirectly addresses this challenge with his contention
that Catholic higher education currently does not operate out of a

comprehensive philosophy of education. He argues that there was a distinctive Catholic philosophy of education prevalent in the United States from the 1930s to the 1960s, but as we entered our contemporary pluralistic era this philosophy faded. Elias claims that a distinctive Catholic philosophy of education emerged out of the nineteenth century.[19] He describes this philosophy of education in different ways. He terms it "Neo-Thomist" because of its reliance on a nineteenth-century rediscovery and interpretation of the philosophical and religious principles of Thomas Aquinas. It also fits the categories of "religious realism" and "religious humanism" because of an emphasis on discovery of abstract principles through the concrete and because of its attempt to connect religious principles with human values.

According to Elias, Neo-Thomism achieved official status in the Catholic church with Pope Leo XIII's 1879 encyclical letter, *Aeterni Patris*. It also was the philosophical underpinning of the 1929 encyclical on education issued by Pope Pius XI. Catholic philosophers and others in positions of authority swore an oath to teach Neo-Thomism. But just as quickly as Neo-Thomism emerged in the late nineteenth century, it departed from the philosophical and educational scene in the 1950s, leaving a philosophical void in Catholic education. More recent work on Catholic education tends to be devoted to a theology of education based on the documents of the Second Vatican Council of the mid-1960s rather than to education based upon philosophical principles.

Neo-Thomists, in Elias's estimation, are closely allied with the neo-rationalist reliance on metaphysics, but the Neo-Thomists insist that metaphysics should be expanded to include the existence of God and the supernatural realm. Neo-Thomist metaphysics not only affirms the existence of unchanging truths about reality and knowledge but affirms that it is only possible to attain the knowledge of this reality through the grace of God. Thus, in Neo-Thomism it is difficult to determine where philosophy ends and theology begins.

*Philosophy of Persons.* According to Elias, the starting point of Neo-Thomism is an understanding of the human person as a rational animal whose highest dignity is found in the intellect and in a personal relationship with God. Human beings constitute the pinnacle of God's creation but remain wounded by original sin. In this view, God creates the human with a body and soul destined for eternal life through the redeeming activity of Jesus, although humans remain free and need to be responsive to this destiny. Human beings, with the grace of God available in the sacraments, struggle to overcome a fallen nature to gain their own salvation and work for the salvation of others. "It is the chief goal of Catholic education to enable persons to achieve the power of mind and will necessary to achieve eternal salvation."[20]

*Social Philosophy*. This view holds that there are two levels of society: the natural level, the province of the family and the state; and the supernatural level, the province of the church. The family has priority over the state on the natural level, and individual good takes precedence over common good when the individual good is of a higher order. Thus, it is the family right and responsibility to educate; only secondarily is it a right of the state. The Neo-Thomists, Elias maintains, make a clear distinction between the primary aim of education—the formation of the person—and secondary aims, such as the transmission of a heritage or a culture, preparation for life in society and good citizenship, and other social aims. They also argue that the formation of the human person should be the primary aim of all cultures.

*Aims of Education*. The essence or aim of education for the Neo-Thomist is "to help persons to make their way on earth by loving God and neighbor, and thus work out eternal salvation by striving for the glory of God both on earth and hereafter in heaven."[21] Closely connected with this aim is recognition of the sinfulness of human beings and the need for grace to overcome this condition. Education must seek to develop students intellectually, morally, and spiritually. There are no explicit social aims of education in Neo-Thomism, only secondary aims. Educated people, in this conception, become intelligent, moral citizens with respect for law.

*Curriculum*. The liberal arts curriculum receives primary emphasis in Neo-Thomism. In this view, a liberal arts education should be for everyone and should contain religious, moral, and ethical dimensions. While practical subjects and even vocational training may be taught, religion is given preeminence in the Neo-Thomist curriculum.

The study of religion and theology forms the heart of Neo-Thomistic philosophy of education. Religious truth and moral formation prevent a narrow concern for this world and guard against a dehumanized life. Religious training in the lower grades should be on a voluntary basis, but it also should be given in connection with the total school environment. In higher education theology should be taught with a sensitivity to pluralism in both secular and denominational institutions.

*Learning and Knowledge.* The Neo-Thomist position asserts that learning is "coming to know the objective reality, the truth."[22] The Neo-Thomist point of view presumes the existence of objective truth concerning God, the nature of human beings, and the nature of the world. Learning, therefore, freely places intellectual virtues in search of truth through the senses, intellect, and will.

*Methods.* A Neo-Thomist philosophy of education does not pre-scribe educational methods; all educational methodologies are al-lowed as long as they do not harm students. Even the methodolo-gies of Progressive education are welcomed if they stimulate students.

*Teachers.* The Neo-Thomist teacher strives to draw out human potential to perfection and activity. Elias explains: "The child is the *material* cause with which the teacher works. The student's activity is the *efficient* cause of learning. The principle of knowledge is within the learner. The *formal* cause or aim of learning is the integrated and liberated human person. The *final* cause is the ideal which the edu-cational achievement presents, that is the vision of God."[23] In a sense, the teacher's role becomes ministerial. The teacher assists the stu-dent in a natural intellectual process in much the same way a physi-cian assists the natural healing process.

## The Decline of Catholic Philosophy of Education

Surveying events over the past forty years makes the reasons for the decline of Neo-Thomistic Catholic philosophy of education seem obvious. John Elias cites a few such reasons. The authoritarian and absolutist stance of many Neo-Thomist tenets make this philosophy implausible in many contemporary U.S. Catholic circles. It resembles a "no salvation outside of the church" stance in theology. Also, the plurality of contemporary movements in philosophy (phenomenol-ogy, existentialism, and many others) calls into serious question the normative stance of Neo-Thomist metaphysics. As Elias points out, contemporary Catholics who are philosophers tend not to term them-selves Catholic philosophers. Also, the Second Vatican Council in the mid-1960s, with its emphasis on freedom and openness to the contemporary world, seriously eroded, if not eliminated completely, the last vestiges of this Catholic philosophy of education.

The picture of U.S. Catholic higher education painted thus far is one in which the experience of Catholics in the first era (1790–1920) dictated distrustful involvement between Catholic education and U.S. culture. The second era (1920–1960) typified Catholicism's version of civil faith, in which the church through education (with higher education at its pinnacle) could transform U.S. culture according to

Catholic spirituality. In a sense, the Catholic hope of this era was that Catholic-educated leaders in U.S. society would transform a predominantly Protestant religious ethos into a Catholic religious ethos. This seemed to be a natural conclusion for a church that had come to identify the tenets of its faith with the ideals of America. Fayette Veverka's dissertation on Catholic schooling in this era is aptly titled "For God and Country."[24] Catholic impressions of both had become almost synonymous by the end of this period, and Catholic education had a Neo-Thomist Catholic philosophy of education in place to carry out the mission. As Catholicism entered the third era (1960 to the present), U.S. culture had not been transformed into a Catholic religious ethos. If anything, U.S. culture has moved from a predominantly Protestant religious ethos to a pluralistic religious ethos. The Catholic philosophy of education predominant in the second era has dissipated along with the passing of the era.

## SPIRITUAL HIGHER EDUCATION

The free exchange of ideas that characterizes the ideals of U.S. higher education often meets with resistance on the campuses of church-related colleges and universities. This resistance finds expression in college-church polity struggles, academic freedom restrictions on theological faculties, and other points of contact in which different conceptions of theology come together.[25] A primary way to find unity in such divergent positions is through attention to educational assumptions that might help church-related colleges and universities articulate a clear and consistent educational philosophy upon which they might plan and operate. This methodological approach resists a forced choice of theological formulations or camps in which a faculty member must pitch his or her tent in order to belong in a church-related college.

### The Search for a Unifying Element

Critics of U.S. higher education point to the lack of a unifying element in secular colleges and universities.[26] Some critics blame the loss of explicit Christian values as the theological and philosophical glue that held higher education together. Others accuse society as a whole for its turn toward secular humanism as its unofficial religious belief system for education devoid of Christian values. Still others denounce the intellectuals in U.S. culture for promulgating their agnosticism and antireligious attitudes in college curricula. No matter who is to blame, critics are correct in asserting that mainstream

U.S. higher education has removed the Christian Bible as the unifying element in education.

Three fundamental changes in contemporary higher education differentiate it from its early denominational beginnings.[27] First, there has emerged in the twentieth century a change in the social theory of education—a movement away from educating the generalist to educating the specialist. Second, emphasis is placed upon science as the way to objective knowledge and truth, so much so that it devalues more imaginative ways of knowing found in religion, literature, and the arts. Third, even though U.S. culture, in part, relies upon educational institutions to provide common social values, the prevailing attitude in U.S. secular higher education seems to avoid or ignore the value-laden dimensions of education and hold to a value-free or value-neutral approach. U.S. higher education has moved from its denominational beginnings with a unified culture of learning to the contemporary fragmented, pluralistic situation. In a sense, U.S. higher education is searching for unifying value and a spirituality of education.

Even church-related higher education has not been very successful at incorporating its religious tradition into its curricula while maintaining academic respectability. Only the most religiously conservative institutions proclaim themselves oriented toward Christian theology and tradition first and academics second. This position is unacceptable to most highly respected Christian colleges and universities. How, then, might a church-related college avoid a doctrinaire, ideological approach to higher education while keeping the respect of the academic community and, at the same time, remaining faithful to its ecclesial roots and faith tradition?

### Spiritual Education: Principles for Church-Related Higher Education

At some point, every academic institution must face the issues of educational purpose, process, context, and structure. With enough reflection, a description of education will emerge from these questions. But rarely are those issues attended to in academic life. Teaching, advising, research, community service, curricula revisions, recruitment and retention, faculty development, and myriad administrative concerns make up much of the college scene. Still, addressing these educational questions has the potential not only for finding unity in a diversity of opinion in higher education, but also for providing a spirituality of education that makes sense for a pluralistic culture.

The principles of spiritual education articulate a framework for the ultimate aim of higher education in general and the distinctiveness of church-related higher education in particular. It seems radical to talk about spirituality in relation to higher education, but that is what higher education needs. Spiritual education, if viewed from a methodological standpoint, reconstructs the founding principles of U.S. higher education as it enters the twenty-first century. Practically and politically, church-related colleges and universities have a greater chance of recovering these principles than do state and private institutions. Yet, this recovery is possible only if there is the will to examine the educational assumptions under which church-related higher education labors.

In order for higher education to be meaning-making, value-laden learning (holistic education), the principles of critical consciousness, authentic community, prophetic action, institutional identity, and spiritual growth must be present. This rather technical description of education points to its complexity. It need not be so technical, however. Good educators innately know when education reaches beyond the mundane. But this innate sense is not enough. College professors and administrators must be intentional in how they structure college life and learning.

The concluding sections of this chapter suggest how spiritual education can transform the rudderless situation of higher education into the holistic education that contemporary critics call for in U.S. culture. By situating spiritual growth as higher education's ultimate aim, church-related colleges and universities can lead the way in the great search for unifying value in U.S. culture. We the People expect spiritual growth to be the ultimate aim of church-related higher education. Not so evident, however, is how these colleges can so deeply influence the social fabric of the United States. These colleges also tend to have a type of split personality in how they deal with the very different realities of academic and social institutions and the church to which they are related.

### Spiritual Growth

Church-related higher education has not been immune to the traditional myth of value-free and value-neutral education. It needs to be reminded that when professor and students engage learning in all of its fullness, questions of value and ultimate meaning are inescapable. It is for this reason that any professor should be able to delve into these meanings out of his or her experience as an academic and as a reflective person generally. The rules of the game, however, should be that the professor must make his or her assumptions and presuppositions explicit to the students. Students then can better understand why the professor holds such opinions. Moreover, students must have the freedom to disagree with assumptions about the nature of the human person and other nondiscipline-related presuppositions. Without an atmosphere of freedom of expression in the classroom, higher education tends to resemble Sloan's *technicism* and *scientism*.

As in all educational settings, church-related higher education involves a process of meaning-making, a way of making sense out of life through the interpretation of experience. This involves more than the accumulation of knowledge, skills, attitudes, and sensibilities. The values inherent in education determine what knowledge, skills, attitudes, and sensibilities are worthwhile to learn. The value question primarily concerns the question of consciousness.[28] The development of consciousness and the parameters it places upon our world determine the values and lifestyles available to us. Thus, meaning-making and valuing are basically different aspects of the same reality. The power of education arises from its formative influence on the learner's consciousness. This means an increase in students' ability to attend to the multifaceted data of their experience, to formulate intelligent understandings about their experience, to judge adequately the veracity and worth of their understandings, and to act responsibly upon their decisions. Education, in great part, introduces this world of meanings to learners as they become ever more familiar with cultural history, science, artistic expression, and the professions. The more varied and detailed are these contexts and meanings, the greater the fund of meanings with which learners might interact.

Holistic education sets the context for human development and transformation. An intellectual transformation can occur when students take charge of their meaning-making, a form of intellectual empowerment. Questions of knowledge and belief naturally lead to questions of value. In moral transformation one moves from decisions based primarily upon satisfactions to decisions based upon values, with a continuing struggle to make those values ever more inclusive. And questions of value lead to questions of ultimate value. Religious, or spiritual, transformation involves being caught in the grasp of ultimate value, and it seems that the role of the educator is to enable learners to identify and explore that transformation. Education, then, is far from indoctrination. It seeks to enable rigorous exploration of all dimensions of life rather than simply presenting objective reality—the answers—for all dimensions of life.

There is a tendency in church-related higher education to segment value considerations into courses such as theology and ethics. This strategy segments this type of reflection into just another discipline to fit into the student's curriculum. No doubt direction and structure should be given to contemplation of ultimate values. This is best accomplished through seminars throughout the student's program of study. Faculty should be recruited to lead these seminars. The closing seminar, the senior seminar, would be an excellent opportunity for students to reflect explicitly upon spirituality grounded in their experience of higher education and plans for the future.

### Education as Social Interaction

U.S. church-related colleges and universities, as social institutions, articulate and contribute to the social values that form the fabric of U.S. culture. Social interaction can be viewed in terms of an educational community and, more broadly, in terms of the general culture.

*Education and Community*. Knowledge is socially constructed and maintained. We are shaped in part by the beliefs, values, attitudes, and social structures of those who came before us. Thus, higher education is an enculturation into the many aspects of human understanding. Cultural literacy movements point out the importance of knowing the flow of culture. But whose culture? Given the global perspectives that characterize this era, even the pervasive influence of Western culture is limited. Moreover, minorities within U.S. culture challenge the interpretation of cultural success that has been handed down by the "victors." Nevertheless, one cannot criticize what one does not know. U.S. higher education is at a crossroad. The challenge is to find ways of familiarizing students with a sense of heritage in Western culture as well as an appreciation of its limitations, and an awareness of contributions of other cultures. The notion of educational community now takes on global perspectives.

Historian-theologian Thomas Berry challenges us to extend the notion of community beyond our social and cultural constructions. He maintains that many of our current difficulties stem from our self-alienation from the natural world.[29] We deny the very context that sustains us when we discount the environment as a partner in the great cultural conversation. The problem, of course, is that the environment cannot speak for itself other than through the death of species and habitat. Higher education is in a unique position to add this voice to public discourse before it is too late.

Higher education, and indeed all education, has a dual responsibility. Its task is not only to pass on cultural tradition but also to promote the critique and progress that come from new ideas, discoveries, and perspectives. We all are involved in a web of meaning that shapes our concept of self and world. The fabric and texture of that web can be made quite explicit by education, and the most effective education comes from communities dedicated to education. But not all educational settings are communities. Community emerges only from the attainment of common meaning, with education integral to the process.[30] Educators make accessible the common fund of knowledge, values, and aspirations of the community. The best educators are thoroughly grounded in the community in which they educate.

The strength of common meaning and purpose can also be a liability to educational communities. Even the best communities have a limited perspective. Our approach to life and education is influenced by the biases of our community needs and values. The best communities make those needs and values explicit in the educational enterprise.

*Education and Public Life.* Education, therefore, is a complex process from both individual and social perspectives. Various educational institutions of society influence individual striving to make sense out of life. These institutions help guide this process in a mix of complementary and conflicting ways by promoting both comparable and contradictory meanings and values. Laurence Cremin suggests three ways to understand educational ecology.[31] First, comprehensively, not only do schools and colleges educate, but many other social institutions educate as well: mass media, the work place, church, governmental bodies, libraries, museums, and so forth. Moreover, a comprehensive approach views education as occurring throughout the life cycle. The neat divisions of elementary, secondary, and higher education fall short of describing the totality of education in an individual's life.

Second, relationally, educational policies and programming should take into account interactions among social institutions, that is, the ecology of social institutions. Thinking nonrelationally places the entire burden for education on schools and colleges. Such thinking ignores the overwhelming influence family life has on students, not to mention the pervasive and influential power of mass media, church, and other social institutions. Relational thinking involves fostering in their students an awareness of the educational power that many social institutions have on their lives.

Last, we must think publicly about education. Public discourse, unfortunately, has tended to be adversarial through the courts and regulatory bodies. Cremin suggests that John Dewey's concept of the politics of persuasion and the quest for community offer a better framework for public dialogue about the means and ends of education. There must be room in a democratic society for individuals to pursue their personal dreams and, at the same time, participate in the continuing quest for community.[32]

In effect, Cremin calls for a great public dialogue about education that asks U.S. citizens, What knowledge, values, skills, and sensibilities do we hold, and what kind of society do we want our children to live in? These questions confront not only schools, colleges, and universities, but they also confront We the People.

Cremin's position on the need for social discourse on the aims and goals of education has both classical and Deweyan aspects. He reminds us of a remark made by Dewey on his ninetieth birthday, "Democracy begins in conversation."[33] And Cremin adds to that dictum Aristotle's contention of two thousand years ago that when we educate we aim at the good of life, and since men and women disagree on their ideas of the good life, they will disagree on their ideas about education.

The idea of public conversation on the good of life and on educational policy promotes the need for a community of communities. Engaging in a dialogue of communities seems to be a more fruitful, albeit more difficult, approach to discussion of the connection between the good of life and public policy toward education. There emerges from such a dialogue different perspectives on the purpose of education from the perspective of different U.S. communities and institutions. This approach contrasts to a lowest-common-denominator approach that results in minimalist aims of education (basic skills) and confused public education policy.

### Church-Related Higher Education and Social Values

There has been, in the United States, a reversal of roles between church and higher education.[34] A primary function of the college, in the colonial era, was to provide a learned clergy for different denominations, and it maintained that the purpose of scholarly work and knowledge was to serve God. The college served a need of the church. Since those eighteenth-century beginnings, there has been an explosion of knowledge and an accompanying emancipation of higher education from church authority. In many ways, we have fulfilled the dream articulated by Jefferson and Franklin of living in an open society freed from the tyranny of an established church.

Voluntary institutions form much of the new order, and higher education plays an important role in providing its social values.

A problem arises with making such claims about the emancipation of education in the United States because they assume a unity of knowledge, integrating framework, or comprehensive foundation for higher education. Does higher education have the ability to provide such unity? As a solution to this problem, Clark Kerr calls for an orientation and organization of the university according to a spirit of inquiry and a continuous investigation of truth, goodness, and beauty.[35] It is the rare university that has the ability to address such philosophical and spiritual issues, much less come to agreement on them.

Alfred McBride takes a more theological or ecclesial stance.[36] He maintains that Catholic higher education (and, one might add, church-related higher education in general) should shed any semblance of value neutrality and be willing to address the moral issues confronting contemporary society. The identity of Catholic higher education, according to McBride, is to be found in the way it deals with moral dilemmas. U.S. society is continually addressing moral issues, but U.S. higher education tends to refuse to deal with them. He goes so far as to state, "Unfortunately, there is some evidence that academia itself may be more a mirror than a prophetic critic of the culture."[37] This is quite an indictment of higher education, given the Cremin contention that prophesy constitutes the essential public function of the educator.

McBride contends that for Catholic colleges an answer to the value-neutral stance demands a commitment to two nonnegotiables: first, there should be systematic approach to theology in the curriculum that fosters a horizon of moral judgment; and second, there should be a restoration of the liberal arts. Catholic graduates need a foundation in theological tradition so that they might develop a framework, a perspective, for moral questioning and deciding. The liberal arts approach better ensures a comprehensive framework to situate specializations and professional education. McBride challenges Catholic higher education with a quote from Albert Einstein:

> It is essential that the student acquire an understanding of and a lively feeling for values. He must acquire a vivid sense of the beautiful and the morally good. Otherwise he—with his specialized knowledge—more closely resembles a well-trained dog than a harmoniously trained person.[38]

These nonnegotiables of becoming grounded in faith tradition and cultural tradition, in McBride's estimation, bear greater potential for the holistic education of persons.

One gets the sense from McBride that Catholic colleges and universities have subscribed to the value-free or value-neutral approach to higher education and have abandoned much of the power of their religious tradition to make meaning in the contemporary situation. Church-related colleges and universities that have downplayed religious tradition for the sake of value-neutrality in the name of rigorous academics have created a dualism between moral value and knowledge and between religion and life. Paradoxically, these institutions initially came into being presumably to break down the very same dualisms they have perpetuated.

### Church-Related Higher Education and Institutional Identity

In order for church-related colleges and universities to be full partners in the cultural search for values, they need to find ways of connecting their concept of education with their concept of church. This reflection is necessary in order to clarify institutional self-understanding and institutional identity in U.S. culture.

Connections between church polity and institutions of higher education are many and varied. In many ways church bodies are very different from U.S. institutions of higher education. Notions about revealed truth, authority structures, and community life differ greatly. In order for church-related institutions of higher education to participate in the dialogue on social values, institutional issues need clarification not only for the sake of self-understanding on the part of these colleges but also for a better understanding in the wider culture about the nature of the college's connection with church.

*Juridical Distinctions.* In the Catholic context, Ladislaw Orsy makes useful distinctions between universities as "Houses of Intellect" and universities as Roman Catholic institutions.[39] Orsy contends that universities as "Houses of Intellect" serve society as institutions supporting and promoting the "operations of the human mind in acquiring and communicating knowledge."[40] Universities promote the competent gathering of data, sound analysis, clear philosophical speculation, and other ways of engaging in disciplined thinking. This emphasis on the human intellect does not mean that the human person is intellectually disembodied from the neck upward. Meaning, values, and social interaction are needs of the whole person. But how can an institution of higher education be both Catholic and a university?

From the perspective of a church theologian and canon lawyer, Orsy makes three helpful assumptions about Catholic institutions of higher education.[41] First, the humanity of the institution needs to be affirmed and respected. Second, the freedom of these institutions to develop a religious dimension should be upheld. Third, the freedom of the Roman Catholic Church to reach out to human institutions and establish various degrees of association or union with them should be recognized. Orsy makes a clear distinction between church and university. Many consider the church divinely inspired, and the university makes no such claim. He also calls for the right of secular institutions to develop explicit religious dimensions as part of their educational mission. He recognizes that a church enters into a relationship with an educational institution in more than one way.

With the exception of a couple of Pontifical Catholic universities in the United States (The Catholic University of America, for example), most U.S. Catholic colleges and universities have an institutional connection with church hierarchy that can be best described as communal.[42] The principle of communion, as opposed to legal incorporation, provides a way for these U.S. institutions to function as both academic and church-related institutions. Orsy does not use the term *communion* in a pejorative sense. He argues that communion, *koinonia* in Greek, provided the powerful force that kept Christian communities together for centuries in the early life of the church. It was not until the twelfth century that powerful legal structures developed. The existence of varying canonical connections between church and university affirms a plurality of possible types of church-university relationships. A clear church-college identity, in turn, adds a clear institutional voice to the cultural search for values in U.S. higher education.

*The Question of Academic Freedom.* Another aspect of clarifying the relationship between church and college deals with the concept of academic freedom. The question of academic freedom in church-related institutions of higher education perpetuates an issue of longstanding debate in the United States. Davis traces the development of academic freedom in the United States back to its roots in eighteenth-century Germany.[43] The German society of the time was such that the university provided greater freedom of expression *Lehrfreiheit* (academic freedom) in the classroom in the informed pursuit of truth than did society at large. This notion of academic freedom, with its accompanying procedural guarantee of tenure, was brought to the United States amid much opposition. Opponents argued that tenure gave institutions too much autonomy and discriminated against nontenured faculty. In reaction to university professors opposing the United States' entry to World War I, objecting to religious conformity, and voicing opinions about sexual morality and race relations, societal opposition to tenure rights and academic freedom continued. Fifteen university professors in 1915 proposed a "Declaration of Principles" on academic freedom and set up procedures to ensure the right of academic freedom. Over the years discussion on the principles continued in various university-related groups and culminated with the 1940 "Statement of Principles on Academic Freedom and Tenure" and three "Interpretations." Numerous organizations have endorsed the 1940 statement, including The American Catholic Philosophical Association in 1952, The College Theology Society in 1967, and the American Academy of Religion in 1967.

The thrust of Davis's study emphasizes his argument with the limitations placed on academic freedom by the 1915 statement, which recognized the need for church-related universities to impose upon their faculties doctrinal standards of a sectarian character. The only stipulation dictated by the 1940 statement is that universities imposing these limits need to state them at the time a professor is hired. The rationale supporting this limitation argues that the study of religion is more subjective or experiential than any other field or discipline and that the religion professor must practice the religion himself or herself in order to teach it competently. Furthermore, an institution should not be required to continue employment of someone who questions or criticizes the institution.

Davis argues with both aspects. He asserts that, first, one must distinguish between subject matter and subject. If the subject matter of a religion is subjective religious experience, then one must distinguish between the analysis or study of this distinctive religious experience and the experience itself. Davis somewhat sarcastically asks, "Participating in a lynching is undoubtedly a subjective experience. Should a study and interpretation of lynchings be dismissed on the grounds that its author has never participated in a lynching? Obviously, not."[44] Second, while an institution has the right not to employ its critics, the nature of a university is the search for the truth in all areas of its purview. If a university grants academic freedom to all other areas of the university and excludes professors of religion from that freedom, such a situation calls into question the commitment to academic freedom in the rest of the university.

Davis's argument with the current limitations of academic freedom placed upon professors of religion raises interesting questions for institutional policy and particularly for the teaching of religion in academic settings. He concludes his study with the observation that in the United States judgment of the correct approach to this problem lies in the perception of the intellectual and ethical consistency or inconsistency of university practice on the part of students, faculty, and the public.

*The Student Nexus.* In reflecting on possibilities for future church-university relationships in the United States, Martin Marty makes five assumptions about the future.[45] First, he contends that efforts to forecast the cultural context of higher education are futile beyond one generation. Second, church-culture relations will not remain static. Third, in all likelihood nothing on the present cultural or ecclesiastical scene and nothing forecasted will make life easier for church-related colleges. Fourth, church-related colleges are among the few bridges between communities of learning and communities of faith. Last, even though the models of church-college relationships are limited, the variations are infinitely rich.

The pace of change is staggering. Marty cites sixteen significant cultural changes that occurred in the United States between 1960 and 1978. Examples include Evangelicalism, Pentecostalism, the appearance of Eastern and occult faiths, the revived women's movement, the cultural awareness of revived Fundamentalism, the Second Vatican Council, and Roman Catholicism's seismic internal shifts. One might add to Marty's list other significant cultural shifts since the late 1970s, for example, the predominance of political conservatism, tremendous advances in computer technology, signs of significant ecological distress, the breakup of the Communist bloc, and many other global and cultural changes.

Marty also describes U.S. culture as viscous, volatile, pluralistic, and one in which nothing lasts. He cites five examples of shifts in religious thought and practice in U.S. culture from the 1960s to the late 1970s: a higher value placed on personal experience, a trend toward authoritarian religion, a low premium placed on theology and religious thought, a lower valuation on common Christian activity, and an underestimation of the secular. These shifts of U.S. culture still seem very plausible as we enter the twenty-first century. One might hypothesize that church bodies (and universities) are now responding institutionally to these changes. Because of the fluidity of cultural change, church-culture relationships must always be changing.

Because of these many changes in U.S. culture, a great number of small church-related colleges have closed over the past thirty years. The surviving colleges struggle with reduced enrollment and its accompanying financial problems. Marty contends that it is important for these church-related colleges to survive because they constitute bridges between communities of learning and communities of faith in U.S. culture. There are few, if any, other ways of relating these two communities. The seminary concerns itself primarily with professional education. Campus ministries on private and secular campuses are primarily ecclesial expressions of church presence. Professors in higher education religion departments tend not to have sustained contact with church polity and interests. Marty proposes that the connection between the church-related college and the college-related church be covenantal—one of mutual respect within a communion of faith.

Marty presents his five assumptions about the future of church-related colleges to give a context to his proposal for relating church and college. Instead of focusing on a particular system of organizational analysis to clarify the identity of colleges and church bodies, Marty suggests that students form the nexus, the link, between church and college. His proposal is not born out of an overly romanticized notion of education and church. He points out that research on church polity and college organization often suggests that people and relationships form the identity and character of organizations. This most often is referred to as "critical mass." In terms of church-college relations, then, critical mass should be composed of caring (interested and informed) people in churches, administration and trustees, faculty members, and students. The constituency most often left out of discussions of church-college relations is the students. This probably is the result of memories of student protests in the 1960s and a form of paternalism, as well as the fact that student bodies tend to be rather undefined and transitory. Marty points out, however, that student populations can coalesce around social issues (for example, war, equal rights) and render a significant amount of power.

Marty draws his proposal mainly from Ortega y Gasset's work on the mission of a university.[46] Even though Ortega y Gasset wrote in a different period and culture, he contends that in order to carry out its mission as a bearer of culture a university must develop a "culture faculty" to carry on an interdisciplinary conversation organized around the themes and concerns of the culture. Marty extends this notion beyond the faculty to the idea of a "culture student body." These students, who Marty contends are readily identifiable by their extracurricular activities, are those who carry the flavor, the style, and the attitudes of the college into the world and into the church. These students and graduates embody church, culture, and college in their own unique ways. The development of these "relators" could also be extended to curriculum considerations in colleges and program formation in churches.

## CONCLUSION

Church-related colleges and universities are in a good position to address many of the value-oriented critiques of contemporary U.S. higher education. But this position is minimized if church-related colleges cannot articulate how education is fundamentally different in their institutions. The tenets of spiritual education can help articulate the difference. Moreover, a U.S. pluralistic culture demands an articulation that makes sense to people outside the religious tradition to which these colleges are connected. A primary way for church-related higher education to address the spiritual hunger of popular culture and maintain the respect of academia is for each college to formulate an educational philosophy that accommodates the values of academic life and church life. The foregoing educational principles give pointers to such a formulation, which, in turn, makes the search for unity in the diversity of opinion of church-related higher education seem more likely.

Utilizing the principles of spiritual education, one can make the case that church-related higher education should be value-laden, meaning-making learning that encompasses five interrelated realities: critical consciousness as a process of holistic intellectual and spiritual human development through prophetic action that occurs best in a communal context, with the human good as a comprehensive purpose in view, under the auspices of an institutional structure, with spiritual growth as its ultimate aim. This conception of church-related higher education accommodates academic and religious value in that it presents an epistemological radicalism that rejects a value-free orthodoxy and supports a critical stance toward the many paradigms of truth and morality in culture.[47] This experience-based process of human development is grounded in spiritual education. The communal context of education asserts the interpretive power of learning communities, as Cremin and Dewey (among others) so eloquently remind us. A comprehensive educational purpose recognizes the need for direction. Lonergan maintains that the human good should be the aim of education, and that development of human apprehension and choice toward the good are the means to making it a reality, a way of progress in culture.[48] The human good, however, is not meant in an exclusive sense. Ecological movements remind us of the good of the earth and nonhuman life and the intimate connection between humanity and the rest of the world and beyond. Institutional structure recognizes the benefits and liabilities of organizational arrangements. The organizational structure of a college better ensures its stability and longevity. Structure, as Orsy and Marty remind us, also needs flexibility to adapt to changing environments. And, as Davis points out, fairness and the freedom of expression of faculty should be upheld in the organizational life of the institution in order for ideological oppression to be avoided. Indeed, church-related higher education can contribute immensely to feeding the spiritual hunger of contemporary U.S. culture. But higher education cannot and should not try to replace the power of church communities. The concluding chapter gives hints on how parishes and congregations can become powerful change agents in the United States by simply fulfilling their central mission—the facilitation of mature spirituality.

# Chapter 8

# A Church at Risk

✝

It was the mid-1960s. The black family entered the church the same way they always had, except that they did not sit in one of the back pews. They continued down the aisle and moved into the second pew. Everyone around them reacted, some with smiles and others in red-faced anger. "They were out to make trouble," one of the church ushers later told the new pastor. "That's why they were beaten in the parking lot after the service," he said matter-of-factly. The young pastor was horrified.

Dan was assigned to St. Ignatius Parish with only the warning that there had been "some racial trouble." "Trouble is not the word for it," he thought to himself as he looked at the dutiful usher. "What happened to those poor people? Did anyone call the police? Were there any lasting injuries? How could this happen?" Dan's anger started to rise as the shock began to wear off.

"Look, Father, we don't want trouble. It's just that colored people should go to colored churches," the usher calmly said. "It's like a private club. You only want people like yourself as members."

"But don't you understand how unchristian racism and violence are?" Dan asked.

"Father, you deal with religious things. I deal with real life. This is politics that we're talking about. And I can tell you that we don't want politics preached from the pulpit," the usher said with a hint of menace in his voice.

Dan flashed back to the incident as he stood outside of the church. He did not know why. Perhaps it was the church burnings on the morning news. Dan had spent the past thirty years at St. Ignatius as pastor. He often thought that it had been the happiest and hardest time of his life. The parish had matured under his guidance. Dan was proud of this community. Now Dan had been assigned to another parish.

Dan spent most of his first few years at St. Ignatius trying to heal the wounds of a racially divided community. In the three-year period prior to Dan's arrival, black membership at St. Ignatius increased from 5 percent to 25 percent. The racial hysteria of the times fed fears among white parishioners that black people would not only take their jobs but their churches as well. Dan worked hard to make racism so obvious a sin that the parishioners would be motivated to overcome it in their parish and neighborhood. It took four hard years to start seeing results. In fact, church attendance initially dropped by 30 percent, but slowly rose back to its original level.

Dan's vision for the parish was quite simple. He vowed to make spirituality the heart of parish efforts. Racism was a primary target, but it was just one way in which spiritual growth was being blocked. Dan's sermons had social implications despite the warning given by the usher who greeted him with news of the beatings. That usher left the parish shortly after Dan welcomed John, a black priest, as assistant pastor. John started a choir dedicated to black spiritual music almost immediately, and liturgical music came alive under John's direction. Within two years the parish had three choirs with different styles of music. John invited his liturgist friends to help incorporate music and art into liturgies. Attendance increased, and soon liturgies at St. Ignatius became the talk of the town.

After ten years of struggling as pastor and battling chronic illness that his doctor blamed on stress, Dan vowed to slow down. As he put it, "My body was giving me spiritual direction." In the course of slowing down, Dan discovered that he and John didn't have to lead everything themselves. He put out a call for help to the parishioners. The response was overwhelming. Dan's only stipulation was that the leaders of these volunteer ministries needed to be educated in ministry studies. Two low-cost diocesan programs provided basic formation. Dan found the money to help twelve parishioners obtain their master's degrees at the local Catholic university. The parishioners, in turn, agreed to provide leadership in the parish during their studies and for three years after they received their degrees. Over fifteen different lay ministries began during a three-year period.

Dan jokingly started to refer to himself as semi-retired. He did find himself more and more in the role of facilitator. He also found time to put together a conflict resolution process that came out of his experience of adversaries' finding common ground. He often said,

"If people of good will trust in God and each other, miracles can happen. But good process sure helps."

All of these memories flashed before Dan's eyes as he got into his car for the trip to St. Ursula Parish in one of the suburbs. A tear trickled down his cheek. No one else was in the car. He had come to St. Ignatius alone, and that's the way he left— alone, but changed.

When Dan left St. Ignatius Parish, his assistant pastor became pastor. The parish team, as Dan liked to refer to it, was composed of ten full-time lay ministry professionals. The parish and elementary school had tripled in size. The parish was half-minority populated and included Asian Americans.

After a forty-minute drive to the nicest suburb in the area, Dan stood in front of his new home. St. Ursula Parish would have been considered a reward assignment by most pastors. The bishop made it clear to Dan, however, that this new assignment would be a challenge. He wanted Dan to go into the parish with an open mind. The bishop was certain that Dan was one of the most spiritual people he had ever known, and he was confident that Dan would be up to the task he was about to face.

The parish was suburban, wealthy, and stable. Dan would have two assistant pastors, who seemed quite affable. Tran was from Vietnam, which excited Dan. He had started to get to know the Vietnamese community at St. Ignatius before he left. But to Dan's surprise there was no Vietnamese community at St. Ursula. The other assistant was from Ireland. A sixty-year-old red-faced stocky Irishman—Patrick—had been at St. Ursula for five years. Dan quickly got the impression that Patrick really ran the place. This was the only parish in the diocese with three priests.

The church building was a huge marble structure, the size and look of a cathedral, with award-winning stained glass throughout. Built in the 1970s, the building debt had been completely retired in five years because of multimillion dollar bequests from two parishioner families. The elementary school buildings also were debt-free. The school had just won an educational excellence award. Tuition was expensive, but the education was superb. As Dan looked over the grounds from his well-appointed rectory study, he whispered to himself, "What's wrong with this picture?"

In preparing for the first parish council meeting at St. Ursula, Dan reflected upon his experience at St. Ignatius. His success as a pastor had come about for three reasons. The first had been the orientation of parish life toward spirituality. This seemed obvious enough, but Dan knew how the busyness of running a church parish could actually seem to become more important than its real purpose. Second, he had trusted in the power of music and art in liturgy. He smiled when he thought back to the days when the African-American choir members smiled at his attempt to clap in rhythm. He was always a half-beat off. Third, he had empowered the parishioners in lay ministry through education. More than anything else, that program had transformed the parish into a vibrant community. As soon as Dan started to invest in the education of lay ministers and their programs, longstanding money problems began to dissipate. Dan wondered if these three insights were up to the task at hand.

The parish council meeting was held at the home of the council president. Dan was being welcomed at a dinner meeting at which he was to present his vision for the parish. When Dan arrived a few minutes early, he was offered a cocktail, which he gladly accepted. It looked like the parish council members had been there a while. Dan wondered if he had gotten the time wrong.

The council president, Roland, welcomed Dan and directed him out to the patio. Roland was a tall man in his mid-fifties with dark hair slicked back, but not with fancy mousse. He was an old-fashioned Brylcream man. Roland had inherited his father's law firm— one of the old-line firms in the city. He continued in his father's tradition of concentrating on corporate law for subsidiaries of large multinational corporations and the largest of the local companies. Roland's firm gave the multinationals a local anchor and an image that the in-house attorneys could never provide on their own.

Roland pointed out some of the exotic plants in the garden and gave Dan a brief history of the house. It was no less than a mansion, somewhat reminiscent of the White House. Dan felt a bit out of place amid such opulence.

Roland turned to Dan and said, "Father, we're somewhat concerned about your position on a number of issues. Fr. Frank, our previous pastor, did a good job here until he started taking courses in theology at one of the Catholic universities. I'm afraid we had to report him to Rome."

"You did what?!" exclaimed Dan with a mixture of shock and amusement. "To whom in Rome did you report him, and did you not talk to the bishop about this?"

"We gave the bishop copies of audio tapes of Fr. Frank's sermons and his adult education classes," Roland said matter-of-factly. "And we contacted the cardinal who is head of the Congregation for the Propagation of the Faith in Rome. He is a good friend of ours and a defender of true Catholicism."

"You did what?!" Dan exclaimed again. "Did you have Fr. Frank's permission to audio tape him?"

"A technicality, Father," Roland said with a smile.

"Father, quite frankly it's apparent to us that you have a socialist agenda," Roland said, looking squarely at Dan. Dan felt broadsided. Roland continued. "We don't want a pastor who will confuse the parishioners with liberation theology and his own brand of Catholicism. We want the true teachings of the church that we learned in our catechism before that God-forsaken Second Vatican Council in the 1960s. We want priests and nuns leading our church dressed in the proper habit, not lay people who think that they have some God-given right to do ministry. All they do is give their opinion. We want facts. You know what else, Father? There are many of us who are willing to fight for the true Holy Roman Catholic Church."

Dan could see that Roland was not about to hear any sort of counter to his views. So Dan calmed himself and asked, "You keep saying 'we.' What is the name of your group, and how many people are involved in it?"

"I'm not at liberty to say how many members we have. But I can tell you our name. We call ourselves Lay Defenders of the Holy Roman Catholic Church. We have affiliations with two international organizations that have representatives in the Vatican."

They both drained their glasses in silence and went back into the house.

Dan knew that he had been set up. He knew that everyone inside understood that he had been warned out on the patio. Now he was to come to the dinner table for more of the same. "God, why me?" Dan thought. The menacing character of the moment felt like his encounter with the racist church usher thirty years before at St. Ignatius. Dan didn't know whether to sit down or not. Everyone was looking at him now. He paused, looked back at each of them, smiled, and said, "Let's start with a prayer."

## The Problem

Most adult Christians do not know much about Christianity. Sermons and various sorts of preaching constitute the religious education of the majority of adult Christians who attend church. This is woefully inadequate because preaching is not the same as teaching. Good preaching is a form of exhortation and inspiration. It cannot be good education. There is not enough time during a sermon, and it cannot be as systematic as a good educational curriculum. No doubt one can learn from sermons, but preaching cannot take the place of systematic education.

Most adult Christians, Catholics particularly, also do not know much about Christianity because their religious education stopped in their childhood or teenage years. There has been a great emphasis on the religious education of children and teens in the Roman Catholic Church; the enormous U.S. Catholic school system built in this century emphasized this approach. In part, the system is its own downfall when it comes to adult religious education. Teenagers literally graduate from religious education when they graduate from high school, never to return. In the Catholic system, the sacrament of confirmation occurs sometime between the age of twelve and eighteen, depending upon diocesan custom. The rite of confirmation is viewed as a rite of passage into Christian responsibility. Parents have the idea that their obligation for the religious education of their children is over at that point. Most Catholics do not view ongoing religious education as an adult Christian responsibility. Catholic parishes have placed almost all of their educational resources in support of this system, thereby neglecting adult religious education. Consequently, the theological turmoil that surfaces from time to time in Catholicism has little if any meaning to the typical Catholic. The result for most adults is a mixture of confusion, disgust, and loss of religious bearings, if bearings existed in the first place.

The U.S. Sunday School movement in Protestantism has done a wonderful job with adult Christian education in comparison to that of Catholicism. Protestant Sunday Schools tend to accommodate adult Christian education quite well. But there are still deep problems. In many cases adult programming has fundamentalistic overtones, and the Christian education of children almost always is fundamentalistic. This is because Protestant ministers are particularly vulnerable to fundamentalistic members of their congregation who complain about educational programs. More often than not, the fundamentals have more to do with personal preferences and piety than the fundamentals of faith. It is much easier for ministers, both Protestant and Catholic, to pay more attention to these types of complaints because they come from members who are well connected in the life of congregation. These members seem more pious and traditional because of their complaints. The silent majority of members feel intimidated by the passion of their fundamentalist conviction and seemingly well-informed knowledge about religion. It is much easier to pacify these complaints than to challenge them.

Learning facts about one's religion simply for the sake of knowing facts is not the primary reason for religious literacy. Its basis and purpose are the promotion of mature spirituality. Only a comprehensive approach to Christian religious education is an adequate vehicle for accomplishing this task. Religious education programs that primarily focus upon the acquisition of facts are clearly inadequate. They do not present enough context and rationale. Programs oriented toward inspiration tend to be thin in theological and scriptural substance. Social outreach programs are often devoid of religious and spiritual reflection. Bible-study programs run the whole spectrum from prayer groups to academic study groups. It is clear that no one program can foster mature spirituality in its fullness. All parish and congregational programs need to be coordinated in ways that promote the multifaceted aspects of the search for ultimate meaning in life.

### The Heart of the Problem

There is a lot wrong. Plurality, uncertainty, and anxiety characterize our social and cultural context. Families are having a more difficult time providing the moral glue to keep society together. Political life seems to have fallen apart. Conservative and liberal political warlords have replaced the certainty of Democrat and Republican platforms and politicians. City governments seem to have gone from being corrupt to being hopeless. The security of corporate life has been replaced by a pervasive anxiety about down-sizing. The rush to global competitiveness has driven failed reforms in education. The world peace anticipated as a result of the dissipation of the Soviet threat has actually turned into violent tribalism and ethnic cleansing.

The church, as a divinely inspired social institution expected to address this societal mess, has failed in the eyes of fundamentalistic Christians. Christianity now exhibits the same pluralism and uncertainty as U.S. culture. According to fundamentalists, Christianity has "sold out" to the secular humanism of modernism. In their eyes the church has given way to pluralistic, relativistic, religious experimentalism. And they feel threatened. The anger that wells up in fundamentalistic Christians comes from a sense of loss and deep frustration. The church is supposed to address these problems, and Christian churches seem to be failing. Fundamentalists are right in their argument that churches should be up to the task of addressing the ills of our age. The problem rests not with the "fundamentals" of the Christian message; rather, the problem lies with the articulation of fundamentals of faith and fumbling efforts to connect the message with the needs of our culture.

Indeed, the heart of a huge problem facing Christianity in the United States is the fundamentalistic world view that pervades Christian churches. As discussed in chapter 3, a fundamentalistic world view is composed in part of ahistorical consciousness or selective historical consciousness, a dualistic understanding of the sacred and the secular, a belligerent stance toward the present cultural and religious situation, a literalist interpretation of the Bible, and an apocalyptic vision of the future. Religion, in this world view, functions as a vehicle for obtaining absolute truth from religious authorities amid a pluralistic, uncertain world for the purpose of obtaining salvation. Personal motivations for subscribing to this view of religion tend to be a fear of ambiguity; anxiety about cultural conspiracies threatening religious orthodoxy; a privatized sense of salvation; longing for a closely knit, like-minded community; and the need to discover a new beginning in life (being born again).

### It's Our Problem

It is understandable why many adult Christians subscribe to this religious world view. Fundamentalists have deeply bought into what has been offered. Typical Christian preaching emphasizes clear lessons to be learned from traditional interpretations of scripture and theology; it emphasizes certainty about scriptural interpretations and notions of theology. Institutional church life tends to promote a dualistic understanding of the sacred and the secular. Too often Christians are led to believe that the only way to get in touch with God is through church. Otherwise, why go to church at all? Fear of hell also has been a primary motivator. One goes to church and obeys the dictates of scripture and church law as outlined and interpreted by ministers in order to be saved. The fundamentalistic world view has its origins, its present energy, and its hope for the future in the institutional life of Christianity. Mainline Christianity is reaping what it has sown. Fundamentalistic Christians articulate with a hard edge what they have been taught.

Personal motivations for subscribing to a fundamentalistic religious world view correspond to prevailing institutional trends in U.S. Christianity. The institutional dynamics of Christian churches are such that ambiguity in theological and church matters is avoided. Theologians engaged in theological exploration and speculation do so at the risk of being silenced or censured. Members of the governing bodies of Christian denominations want to control the appointment (and firing) of professors in seminaries and church-related colleges and universities. The authority and faithfulness of dissenting bishops, pastors, and ministers are questioned in the name of religious orthodoxy.

God's love is the mantra of many Christian congregations and parishes. But saving one's soul and avoiding damnation are still primary reasons given for belonging to Christian congregations. The fire-and-brimstone sermon has given way to more subtle ways of letting people know that they are heading to hell if they do not follow the dictates of church customs and interpretations of moral law. Many Christian churches profess to be open to all who want to explore faith and spirituality, but they act too much like like-minded communities. Christian churches continually call members to be born again and begin a new life in the Spirit. It is the unusual church that takes this call to heart itself and seeks new life and new beginnings in its own institutional structures. The fundamentalistic world view outlined above still serves as the predominant influence in church practice today despite advances in theological scholarship and increases in the general educational level of congregations.

## THE CHRISTIAN OPPORTUNITY

America has fallen in love with the sacred. Books on spiritual themes are on best-seller lists in numbers greater than ever before.[1] Tele-evangelism is alive and well. The Christian Right is as active in politics as ever. New Age religious movements of various sorts make headlines. Yet, as previously reported, only 35 percent of Americans can be classified as being religious. In other words, there are millions of people who consider spirituality important. But they cannot find a home for that spirituality in organized religion. If Christianity were up to the task of meeting the spiritual needs of adult Americans, churches would swell with new members and welcome back old members who have lapsed. However, this is not the case.

Christianity is the religious background of the majority of adults in the United States. If Christian congregations and parishes were to meet the spiritual needs of adults, there could be a tremendous Christian awakening as we enter the twenty-first century.

Some institutional soul-searching is in order. Church leaders need to ask themselves if the heart of their pastoral plan is the enablement of mature spirituality. Are their churches inviting all who seek deeper meaning in life? A fundamentalistic approach to religion will attract a portion of the American public to Christian church life, but the vast majority is looking for something else. Herein lies an opportunity for revitalization in Christian churches.

### A Spiritual Approach to Revitalization

Christian spiritual humanism, as an alternative religious world view to fundamentalism, has a real chance of reaching out to a spiritually starving U.S. culture. It can provide an organizing framework for the revitalization of congregational life. Its thrust is outward toward the evangelization of popular culture. As discussed in chapter 4, religion, in a Christian spiritual humanist world view, functions as a vehicle for approaching truth in a holistic way amid a pluralistic, uncertain world in the hope of forging a relationship with God and all of creation. Personal motivations for subscribing to this view of religion are not far removed from those of a fundamentalistic view of religion. There is still fear of ambiguity, anxiety about threats to religious orthodoxy, questions about salvation, longing for community, and the need for a new beginning. The difference is that a Christian spiritual humanist view of religion struggles with those fears in a church community that is open to the God of religious tradition and God's presence in the world. To participate in this type of community is to be part of a vibrant living tradition that seeks growth in the Spirit of God found in all creation.

Spiritual education brings about Christian spiritual humanism in parish and congregational life. The description of Christian spiritual education, as outlined in chapter 6, is intentional meaning-making and value-laden learning that encompasses five interrelated realities: critical consciousness, authentic community, prophetic action, institutional identity, and spiritual growth. This technical definition is only an approximation of the art of spiritual education.

The art of spiritual education is an expression of how a church community organizes itself to meet the spiritual needs of itself and others. It recognizes the intimate connection between spirituality and education. Education is a powerful human endeavor. It gives us a framework to make sense out of the world around us and, at the same time, to increase the complexity of that world to accommodate more possibilities. The cumulative experience of education is like stepping into a hot-air balloon and rising above the landscape. The panoramic view gives a sense of the context in which we live our lives. As the balloon travels to other terrains, we see other possibilities and different landscapes. Yet, they all are connected in the greater context of the earth. Spirituality involves contemplation on the meanings of each of those landscapes in light of their connection to each other and in the context of the earth and the universe.

Education increases the fund of meanings available to human beings to make sense out of an increasingly complex world. Spirituality is the way in which we keep our bearings as we engage more complexity in life. It has a balance of conservative and progressive instincts. In other words, we have a spiritual need to conserve the meanings and values that we hold dear. This stability is comfortable.

When we encounter more complex and problematic situations that challenge those comfortable meanings, however, we need to be able to expand them to accommodate more complete meaning and value. That potential growth situation is uncomfortable. Our comfort level will return only when we can truly take responsibility for that growth.

James Fowler presents a helpful description of the ways in which human beings tend to deal with an increasingly complex world view as they mature. His articulation of different stages of faith, as outlined in chapter 2, gives a good sense of how growth in faith needs to correspond to the growth in intellect and other areas of our lives. Even without assigning it to a particular stage of faith development, it seems clear that a fundamentalistic world view is not in sync with the intellectual development of mature adults. It is not that fundamentalists are intellectually immature people. Quite the contrary. But intellectual ability and achievement are not the issues. The problem is that their religious world view tends not to withstand the scrutiny of constructive criticism. Often fundamentalistic fundamentals of faith are composed of fragile comfort areas that resist expansion and growth. Therefore, an elaborate world view is set up to protect them.

Fowler's use of the term "sacrament of defeat" as almost a prerequisite for the movement into a mature faith (conjunctive faith), is a striking example of the need to test our fragile notions of God and ultimate meanings in order to grow spiritually. The sacrament of defeat means experiencing disappointment at the deepest levels of human experience. The death of a loved one, divorce, being fired from a job, being diagnosed with a life-threatening disease are just a few examples. It entails the feeling that one has been dealt an unfair blow. How could a loving God allow such things to happen? Mature faith embraces such paradox in a way that opens up new possibilities. Truly trusting in God is one way of putting it.

No wonder there is an inverse relationship between levels of education and levels of religiosity—the higher the level of education, the lower the degree of religiosity. A fundamentalistic religious world view has pervaded U.S. Christianity to such an extent that young Christian adults find it difficult to negotiate the movement from a critical examination of faith typical in the late teens and young adult years to a more mature faith. Higher education does a great job of helping students explore foundational assumptions about life and introducing new horizons. But higher education finds it very difficult to help students reconstruct a coherent world view. That reconstruction could be accomplished in Christian church communities, but that has not been the case.

Christian churches seemingly have been unable to help young adults reconstruct their lives for two reasons. First, Christian education has been dominated by apologetics—the branch of theology concerned with the defense of Christianity. Churches are preoccupied with the need to defend traditional beliefs and practices at the expense of fostering reflection on a creative encounter with God. Churches need to find ways of educating children about Christian tradition as an ongoing search for God in our life experience instead of teaching facts and stories as simply deposits from the past. Second, Christian churches tend to focus too much on how easy it is to lose one's faith amid conflicting philosophies, morality, and theologies prevalent in higher education and the work place. Churches should recognize that those encounters are part of living a reflective life and should encourage the exploration of those different perspectives as part of Christian education, not as opposed to it. In other words, Christian education as spiritual education welcomes reflection on all conflicting opinions and philosophies of life as part of an open exploration by people of faith.

### Ministry Education

A key to making spiritual education an important part of pastoral life is the congregation's view of pastoral leadership. Engaging in spiritual education is less possible in a parish or congregation that wants to sit back and have religion provided to them. Likewise, ministerial leaders who view their role as provider will not foster spiritual education. Spirituality is not a commodity to be provided. It is an innate part of the human constitution that blossoms with nurture.

The traditional notion of the seminary is that it should remove clergy candidates from the world to educate and form them in the spiritual life. In effect, this system promotes a dualistic view of church and world. Implicitly the world is viewed as a place to be taken from in order to be holy. Therefore, the world is the place of the temporal and secular, and the church is the place of the spiritual and sacred. The problem, of course, is that Christianity and the world cannot be separated. They are as intimately connected as body and spirit. We are bodily creatures who are spiritual. Human beings are both in the world and of the world, and so is the Christian church. This notion affirms God's graced intentions for the world. The world becomes profane when we theologically take God from it.

A way to avoid dualistic tendencies in clergy education is to make it clear to candidates that one of their primary responsibilities is to help people find God in their everyday lives—in the world. This responsibility necessitates being able to identify with the concerns and struggles of people in U.S. culture. The seminary should be a place that models what parishes and congregations should be about—the promotion of mature spirituality. Learning to overcome fundamentalistic tendencies is a challenge to most Christian seminaries today. Discerning the difference between conservatism and fundamentalism is very important. Seminaries need conservatives and liberals for a healthy balance of perspectives. The intransigence of fundamentalistic attitudes does not allow for such balance.

Largely due to the shortage of priests, lay ministry has become an important part of Roman Catholicism over the past few decades. Most ministerial services today are provided by lay people in Catholic parishes. Sociological data on Catholicism tell us that, excluding the pastor, 83 percent of Catholic parish ministry, either paid or unpaid, is performed by lay women and men.[2] If we focus just upon those parish ministers who are paid, 57 percent are lay persons. About twenty thousand lay people and religious sisters and brothers are employed at least twenty hours a week as parish ministers in half of the nineteen thousand Catholic parishes in the United States. This is in addition to those on the staffs of Catholic schools. Approximately 85 percent of new full-time parish ministers are women, of which 40 percent are religious sisters and 60 percent are lay women, most of whom are married. Almost 40 percent of the religious sisters are over sixty years of age, while only 8 percent of the lay people are over sixty. Thus, in the future, an even higher percentage of Catholic parish ministers will be lay people. Given Catholicism's contemporary situation, it no longer can assign the realm of the sacred solely to clergy and religious and the realm of the secular solely to laity. As we can see from these statistics, 83 percent of parish ministry is performed by lay people. The realm of the sacred today is as much a province of the laity as it is of the clergy in the Catholic church.

Protestant church polity and structures differ from denomination to denomination in regard to lay ministry. Having broader access to the clergy gives most Protestant churches an adequate supply of ordained ministers. Protestant church communities, however, are much smaller than the typical Catholic parish. Therefore, funds to support full-time clergy tend to be fairly tight. Lay ministry is at least as important in Protestantism as it is in Catholicism. In both Catholicism and Protestantism, the education of lay ministers is crucial to the health of Christian churches today. It is unfair and inappropriate to put members of congregations and parishes in leadership positions without appropriate education and skills. The notion of lay people as simply helping the clergy is quickly waning. A distinction should be made between giving assistance and engaging in ministerial leadership. Lay ministers need education and training that gives grounding and skills for leadership in the Christian community. It is just as serious an education as that of clergy education. Not all lay ministers need a master's degree or a doctorate, but they need education that gives them the solid background and skills to carry out their ministry.

<h3 style="text-align:center">LESSONS FOR A CHURCH AT RISK</h3>

We often hear that experience is the best teacher. But that is only partially true. A more complete statement is reflected-upon experience is the best teacher. In these pages I have tried to point out how Christianity is a church a risk because of the religious illiteracy prevalent among adult Christians. Not that children and teens are more literate about their religion, but adults are the decision makers in their churches. We have seen how, despite the increase in educational levels generally in U.S. culture, adults remain comparatively illiterate about their religion. This situation is perilous because of the plurality of different religions in the U.S. as well as the many different opinions within Christian denominations. Religious literacy is needed now more than ever before to make sense out of a changing religious landscape.

Theologian David Tracy characterizes late-twentieth-century culture as dealing with plurality and ambiguity.[3] The plurality of U.S. religious culture is only part of the plurality and ambiguity of all social institutions in this era. The increased availability of higher education over the past thirty years has brought with it the ambiguity found in historical consciousness. Knowledge of history can throw into question bedrock cultural understandings so much so that it can become the "terror of history."

The religious and cultural uncertainty of the times has given rise to the need for grasping hold of that which is certain. Fundamentalism offers a tight, safe world view that provides comfort in the midst of an ever changing environment. The comfort, however, is provided at the expense of further growth in spiritual maturity. Most mainline Christian denominations have incorporated this religious world view into their theology and practice. The paradox for most Christian churches is that short-term growth is to be found in a fundamentalistic viewpoint because those who attend church find comfort in its tenets. The overwhelming majority of Americans, however, do not find solace in fundamentalism. But Christian churches seem not to have much else to offer.

U.S. Christianity's at-risk situation is as much an opportunity as it is a problem. Christianity has the spiritual resources to meet the needs of contemporary culture. What Christian churches choose to focus upon and how they offer the resources of Christian tradition make all of the difference in the world. The following lessons for Christian churches come out of personal experience as well as that of We the People.

## I. Make Spirituality the Heart and Soul of Church Life

The phrase *heart and soul* connotes the coming together of body and spirit. The Christian doctrine of Jesus Christ's being fully God and fully human gives the most complete example of how Christian churches should understand themselves. Just as Jesus of Nazareth was born into the society and culture of his day, so must Christian churches, as followers of Christ, be born into the concerns of each generation in every culture. It is clear that the primary Christian message of God's love for human beings and all creation transcends particular societies and cultures, but that message remains unarticulated if it is not in the language of the people.

The intimate connection between Christianity and the arts has long been recognized. Liturgical music traditionally has been commissioned by church leaders and written and performed by the musical luminaries of Western civilization. Music, sculpture, painting, dance, and poetry have reminded human culture of mystical insight since the beginning of time. Religion would be an empty approximation of the spiritual life without the arts.

Liturgical artistic expression is but a small part of spiritual inspiration that occurs in U.S. culture all the time. Contemporary music, movies, and literature inspire millions of people each day. Evangelical Christians have discovered Christian pop music as a vehicle for inspiration. A Roman Catholic media group gives its version of the Oscar each year to the best feature movie that contains a clear moral message. These institutionally connected expressions of spirituality are but a small part of spiritually charged artistic inspiration in popular culture. The international rock concerts that have been staged to benefit disaster relief efforts accomplish a lot more than raising money. These cultural para-liturgical events bring together people of all types and persuasions in a common bond, a sense of spiritual connectedness, and moral responsibility.

Andrew Greeley, Roman Catholic priest-novelist-sociologist, started writing novels with the conviction that popular fiction has the ability to influence many more people than traditional Christian preaching and teaching. Popular literature containing a spiritual message (and I think all good literature has a spiritual message) has the potential to reach many more people than the 35 percent of the population who consider themselves to be religious. James Redfield's *Celestine Prophecy* has sold millions of copies over the past few years not because of great writing but because it contains a spiritual message that touches the spiritual imagination. Christian churches should be engaged in these types of spiritual outreach, not to control them, but to recognize their influence on the lives and imagination of the public. These expressions of spirituality should be encouraged and used whenever possible to reach people who are not in the pew on Sunday as well as to inspire those who are in the pew.

A primary theological presupposition of Christian spiritual humanism is that salvation is a matter of relationship rather than singular accomplishment.[4] Too often salvation is portrayed as a task to be accomplished instead of a relationship of trust to be entered into. This relationship is pluriform, just as the Christian Trinity is a pluriform expression of God. Salvation is not just a relationship of trust between individuals and God; it includes other human beings and all of creation. This relationship gives us a sense of the holy—a holistic approach to life. We can make decisions and be responsible for them with motivations for the common good of all creation when we take this holy relationship to heart. The attainment of truth is not a singular accomplishment. It is a matter of trusting in the paradigms of truth and morality with which we come in contact throughout our lives. Christianity merits trust, but that is not the point. In order to be relevant in contemporary U.S. culture, Christian churches need to embody and promote trust. In other words, they must act like trusting communities rather than judgmental communities, concentrate on salvation (relationship) rather than damnation, and accept the ambiguities of life instead of trying to explain them away. Contemporary theologians agree that God is ultimately mystery. Radical monotheism is needed now more than ever before. The one true God is above all of our human ideas and approximations of God. The complexity of cultures and the universe is challenging us to let go of antiquated conceptions of sacred certainty. Christianity must be up to the task of promoting responsible trust in a loving God—the substance of mature spirituality.

## II. Make Adult Spiritual Education the Centerpiece
## of Pastoral Planning

Spiritually alive Christian churches orient church life toward sparking spiritual imagination through art, music, literature, and the rest of the arts. But too many churches tend to stop there. Once spiritual imagination is sparked, the task is to help people deepen reflection on their spiritual life. This process obviously is not a once-and-for-all situation. Spiritual insight comes and goes with the ebb and flow of life. Christian churches, therefore, need to be flexible in their programming to accommodate life instead of expecting life to accommodate church.

Spiritual education can be likened to Alfred North Whitehead's rhythm of education. According to Whitehead, human intellectual growth is comprised of three stages or cycles.[5] The first movement is that of romance. Romance is Whitehead's way of expressing the experience of being captivated by a person, idea, or event. We are motivated to know more when our imagination and emotions are aroused. Once romance occurs, the need for the next stage arises—precision. The stage of precision deepens our understanding with information, analysis, and contemplation. Sometimes the romance fades because of analysis and critique. The last stage, generalization, challenges us to accommodate this newfound knowledge into our world view. This stage is like a return to the romance of discovery except that the possibilities and implications for our lives have been refined through the crucible of precision. We can genuinely generalize only about that which we know, moving from the particular to the general and back again.

Whitehead's rhythm of education can be likened to Lonergan's critical method (see chapter 6). The romance stage is like Lonergan's description of experience. When we attend to something particular in our experience, we are captivated and want to know more about it. Whitehead's precision stage is what Lonergan describes in the stages of understanding and judgment. We try to be intelligent in our understandings and reasonable in our judgments. Whitehead's generalization stage is like Lonergan's description of the deciding stage of critical method. Both Whitehead and Lonergan remind us that the romance and emotion of our experience become more precise when we try to be intelligent and reasonable about our experience so that we might generalize, that is, be responsible about our decisions.

Both Whitehead's rhythm of education and Lonergan's critical method offer insight for church ministers. There is a tendency among many ministers to pitch their tent in one of the stages and basically ignore the rest. Preachers and evangelizers tend to be caught up in the romance of spiritual experience and do not (or cannot) invite people into deeper reflection on their experience. Other ministers and Christian religious educators ignore the need for the emotion of religious experience and try to start with precision—Bible study and religious education classes. The worst situation is a church congregation that is ensnared in generalizations that are not fine-tuned by intelligent and reasonable precision and motivated by genuine religious experience. Tele-evangelist shows that are caught up in this type of empty generalization are all the more crass and offensive because of their public exposure.

### III. Empower the Laity

Christianity belongs to the laity. Their faith, trust, finances, and voluntary efforts support church life. Ministry, therefore, should be accountable to them, and it seems only reasonable that it should come from them. Ministers should be servant leaders who profess their service to the community. This is the professional nature of ministry. Religious educator Gabriel Moran reminds us of that ancient meaning of *profession* as one's dedication of education and talents to the service of the community.[6] Unfortunately, the modern notion of profession has come to mean that professionals tend to be more dedicated to their professional associations than to their local communities. Attorneys, health-care professionals, teachers, and even ministers can lose sight of their professed commitment to the community.

Empowerment comes with knowledge and a sense of ownership. The story at the beginning of the chapter provides an illustration. In the story, Fr. Dan and his assistant knew that they could not continue providing all of the ministry to the parish. Yet, when Fr. Dan asked for assistance, he did so only in the context of providing education for lay people to carry out their ministry. Volunteers get burned out with tasks that require education and skills that they do not possess. But they try to carry out the ministry anyway because there is no one else to do it; that is manipulation, not empowerment.

### IV. Accommodate Diversity

Christianity by its very nature is diverse. Differences exist in Christian theology, interpretations of the Bible, religious practices, and types of church communities. Moreover, each church congregation is made up of individuals with very different conceptions of God and church. Theologian Avery Dulles's identification of different models of church reminds us that some church members emphasize the institutional aspects of church, others point to its communal dimensions, yet others envision social outreach as what church should be about, and still others emphasize different models.[7] All of these different models of church are valid because Christian churches indeed have institutional, communal, prophetic, mystical, and evangelical aspects. It is just that some members emphasize one or more aspects over the others. Likewise, theologian H. Richard Niebuhr in his classic book *Christ and Culture* outlines different ways in which Christian church communities understand the relationship between church and culture.[8] Some church members have a tendency to view church as being a part of culture, others view church as being opposed to culture. Some church members understand themselves as being transformers of culture, others perceive church as interpreting sacred reality for culture. Aside from these theological conceptions of church, the stages of church affiliation outlined in chapter 2 remind us that people attend church for different reasons, depending on what is going on in their lives. Indeed, diversity best describes the reality of church life.

A primary task of ministerial leadership is to recognize the diversity that exists in each church community and to orient church life toward accommodating all who attend. This is easier said than done. Another way of stating the task is that ministers need to find unity in the diversity of church life. The unifying element most appropriate for church life is the promotion of mature spirituality. In other words, church life should be oriented toward the many ways in which people seek deeper meaning in life—being able to reflect spiritually on life's complexities.

Church members are at different stages of faith development and different life situations. Ministry, therefore, is a matter of determining individual needs and finding ways to address them. This approach to ministry is time and personnel intensive. But, paradoxically, the search for spirituality is a communal endeavor. An atmosphere of tolerance can pervade Christian church communities by simply recognizing the differences in people who have a common quest for spirituality.

The unifying element in church life is not proclamation of answers to life's problems. Unity should come from the common search. Christianity gives a framework for that search. While many of today's problems are unique to the lives of individuals and the era and place in which they live, Christian tradition contains universal spiritual themes (death, salvation, suffering) with which human beings have been dealing throughout the ages. Putting congregation members and the culture-at-large in touch with this vast and diverse spiritual resource is one of Christianity's greatest challenges. But that is only part of the total equation. Christian churches need to be open to the diverse and sometimes profound resources that come from others in the wider culture who also are on the search for spirituality. Dealing with diversity from within church communities and from outside in the popular culture forms one of Christianity's greatest challenges, and, at the same, time one of its noblest callings.

### V. Embrace Technology Cautiously

The great cathedrals of antiquity, in part, were attempts to root Christianity in the culture of the era. Engineering and architectural breakthroughs went into the construction of those magnificent churches. Christianity had little difficulty in embracing those technologies. Technology is much more complicated today, and Christian churches can embrace it, reject it, or ignore it. The more fruitful approach is to embrace it.

Historian of technology John Staudenmaier contends that technology is one of the signs of our time.[9] He points out that two different sets of symbols characterize contemporary culture's view of technology. One set emphasizes the liberating aspects of technology. Science and technology free us from many diseases and enable us to travel, build, communicate, and create in ways that were unimagined in the past. These high-tech symbols are very attractive to us. The other set of symbols, however, paints a very different picture—disintegration. Crumbling highways clogged with automobiles, cities filled with smog and crime, weapons capable of unimaginable destruction, and impersonal computer systems are among the many examples of how technology has turned out to be harmful, if not disastrous. Moreover, as theologian-historian Thomas Berry contends, earth has become sick as a result of runaway technology, and human beings are not likely to remain well on a sick planet.[10] This second set of symbols points out the dark underside of technology's wonders.

Philosopher of technology Timothy Casey points out that current labor-saving technological advances that are supposed to give us greater leisure in our lives have actually increased the amount of time we spend working.[11] In the Middle Ages, people typically worked only one-half of the year. The Industrial Revolution lengthened the work day, and we now consider two to four weeks of yearly vacation time to be a good employment benefit. No doubt there are huge differences in our standard of living today. But one might even question that, given the prevalence of stress in our lives. Technology, therefore, has brought many wonderful things to us. But we both revere and fear it. Our challenge is to create and use technology reflectively. If we do not, it can have disastrous consequences.

Technology is not simply a category of tools that we use for good or bad. It is part of what shapes our world. Professor of communications Paul Soukup, S.J., claims that we make technology a transparent extension of ourselves.[12] For example, we extend our hearing with the telephone and our seeing with telescopes and microscopes. Computers extend our senses and computational abilities in a number of ways. Technology is transparent because we do not have to know how devices operate in order to use them.

Soukup contends that technology shapes our attitudes and language. The telephone has become such an important part of our lives that when it rings at home or in an office, a conversation between two people in the room will almost always be interrupted. Soukup claims that "we borrow from technology to describe ourselves. Our minds become computers with inputs and outputs; things 'do not compute,' people 'interface' with one another; we process information or just plain 'process.'" Language is a primary way in which we name and construct reality. But the reverse is also true. Language subtly shapes our reality. The same is true of technology. We use it to shape and control our world. But in turn it, in part, determines cultural reality.

Church communities can utilize contemporary technology both to reach out to the popular culture and to help people reflect upon how technology affects their view of reality—even ultimate reality. Some independent preachers and churches have used technology quite effectively over the past few decades. Jimmy Swaggart supposedly had a state-of-the-art computer system over a decade ago for keeping databases of current and prospective donors to his various ministries. Television and radio have been and continue to be media for Christian evangelists. Bible tracts and even the mass production of the Bible by the Gideons are products of modern print technologies.

Mainline Christian churches, however, have been reticent about embracing technology to the same extent as tele-evangelists and some churches. Mass media seem to be most effective for fundamentalistic types of programs that rely on short, simple, clear messages and "sound bytes." More substantive and complex types of religious programming have been less successful. There are at least five ways of addressing this issue.

First, Christian churches can use television, radio, and other mass media to good advantage if programming is oriented toward inspiration. Crassly put, there is entertainment value to telling stories of faith and transformation. People are captivated and moved emotionally by stories of spiritual awakenings so long as the production of such programming is as good as other dramatic programs. Feature movies should be considered as well. Media can affect and influence the popular culture in ways that traditional church services cannot approximate. These programs, however, should not be substitutes for church services, which leads to the next point.

Second, technology should be used to enhance church life. Good use of technology can enhance church ceremonies and services of all types. Just as artistic expression is an integral part of inspiration, so the use of technology can make church ceremonies more accessible to the parish or congregation. No doubt there are limitations placed upon some ceremonies by the traditions of particular Christian denominations, but there is usually a significant amount of flexibility in how services are presented. Multimedia technology can be both tasteful and inspirational.

Third, the use of technology can enhance church administrative and educational services. Computers can keep databases for mailing lists, survey results, newsletters, and other publications. Churches can create home pages on the World Wide Web to provide information on upcoming events and to provide e-mail access to ministers and other church members. Telecomputing and other technologies also can be used to provide in-depth information and education to church members and to the public at large. Universities now offer courses on the Internet at all levels, and the technology to offer such courses is becoming more and more accessible. Print materials, video, and audio can be put on the Internet for people to receive and interact with at their leisure. Small-group "meetings" could then be held to discuss the material and its implications for participants' lives.

All of these uses of technology can enhance church life. Embracing technology also keeps ministers in touch with the pulse of the culture. Ironically, use of technology gives Christianity in the United States the potential to evaluate most effectively technology and other foundational aspects of culture. Over the airwaves and through cable lines Christian leaders can point out the potentially deadening effects that unreflective use of technology can have on our lives. Indeed, it is important for Christian churches to embrace technology, but it must be done cautiously.

## VI. Imagine Jesus in Our Midst

In these pages I have tried to outline the crisis situation that U.S. Christianity faces in the late twentieth century. Theologically, the legacy of the distancing of Christian theology from the people over the past two thousand years has made its mark. In effect, we have been experiencing the distancing of God from the popular culture.[13] Psychologically, the anxieties of our era heighten the desire for certainty, trust in authority, and the need to deal with an increasingly complex life situation. Sociologically, mainline Christian churches have been experiencing decreased attendance rates in the second half of this century, while fundamentalistic churches are experiencing increased attendance. Christian activists have entered the political area with mixed success and with ambivalence about Christianity's role in society—politically neutral or politically active. Spiritually, U.S. Christianity faces a crisis of faith. The hunger for spirituality is as strong as ever, yet the majority of people in U.S. culture are not finding that hunger fulfilled by traditional Christian churches.

The way to address this crisis is not to condemn U.S. culture as a whole. The answer lies not solely in the creation of alternative Christian churches and spiritually oriented organizations. The answer lies in the mutual spiritual education of Christian churches and U.S. culture. I believe that the majority of Christians in the United States long for familiar mainline Christian churches to reach out in ways that make sense to them. This outreach requires, on the part of churches, an appreciation and a respect for the noblest aspects of U.S. culture.

Just as this book started with stories of awakenings, I offer a different type of awakening story in conclusion. I received a telephone call from a friend early one morning who said rather excitedly, "I had a dream last night that I think you should hear about." Colleen had a habit of keeping track of her dreams. She claims that dreams help us understand deep feelings, emotions, and thoughts that sometimes get covered up by the control mechanism that we place upon our consciousness. "Anything is possible in a dream. That's what makes them so wonderful," she often says. Colleen had been a religious educator for over twenty-five years when I first met her. To know Colleen was to know that she was an educator through and through. According to her, "Good educators are always dreamers."

The daughter of a first-generation Irish Catholic family from Chicago, it was presumed by her family that Colleen would enter the convent. To her parents' disappointment, she entered college instead and became an elementary school teacher. After three years in education, she decided to enter the convent in the late 1960s. She fulfilled her parents' dream, but on her own terms.

Colleen seemed to counter the religious trend of the era. She entered the convent at a time when many sisters were leaving it. Colleen continued teaching elementary school in one of the order's inner-city schools. It was challenging but rewarding for a few years. But then she became restless and wanted to expand her ministry from teaching school to pastoral ministry. Her college degree was in elementary education, so she attended a pastoral studies graduate program in a Catholic university to study theology and pastoral ministry. Colleen worked as a director of religious education in a Catholic parish. She liked her ministry immensely, especially the two-week adult education classes that she and the pastor offered twice a year.

Colleen wanted to expand her ministry even further, however. She petitioned her religious order superior to become a consultant for adult religious education in a Catholic diocesan office of religious education. She received permission to pursue the position. Colleen received the offer but turned it down. Exasperated, her superior asked why.

"I do not know enough about adult education," Colleen replied.

"But the diocesan officials think that you do," her superior shot back.

"Please give me one year to take courses on adult education at the state university. This will be my last request for higher education."

Colleen's superior rubbed her temples and simply said, "Yes, but God help me."

Colleen spent one year studying the principles of adult education in a graduate program at the state university nearby. She was the only religious sister in her classes, which pleased her. Colleen learned a lot from her professors as well as from her fellow students who taught in public schools and from other students who held human resource development positions in corporations. They all were enamored with Colleen, who openly talked about spirituality.

After completing her studies, Colleen applied for a position as adult religious education consultant in another Catholic diocese. She spent her first two years helping parish directors of religious education find appropriate curricula and bringing in guest speakers on adult learning. Her efforts seemed to be going nowhere, however. A breakthrough came when she encountered Fr. Dan's parish (the story at the beginning of this chapter). Fr. Dan trusted his director of religious education enough to allow her to form study groups in the parish. Groups of eight to twelve adults gathered to study the Bible, church history, current events, parenting, and various areas of spirituality. Colleen set up a training program for facilitators in the parish to lead the groups. The groups met in their homes and occasionally called upon Sr. Colleen and Fr. Dan to speak to them about topics that seemed unclear. After two years the parish became an even more vibrant community. As one of the parishioners put it, "Religion is starting to make sense to me, and I want my children to know about it."

Sr. Colleen and I had wonderful talks over the years about her program. There was a crisis when Fr. Dan left the parish, but the new pastor, Fr. John, continued and even expanded religious education. I had been working with Colleen on a writing project over a six-month period before she called that morning.

She began her description of the dream.

> "In my dream I was staffing an exhibit booth for a publishing company at an ecumenical religious education conference. I couldn't quite figure out why I was there other than I was asked to substitute for the publishing company's adult religious education consultant who normally covered such events. The exhibit area was set up as usual in a large room of the hotel in which the conference was taking place. Everything seemed typical. There were about fifty different exhibitors—publishing companies and other firms that service churches of various denominations. But atypically, the conference attendees were only senior church leaders—bishops, presidents, and national church officials." Colleen was amazed by all their different types of regalia. They passed by her booth and politely nodded but did not stop to talk with her. As the day wore on, she became frustrated.
>
> Finally, right before closing time, one of the church officials stopped by and spoke to her. "Sr. Colleen, I have been using an adult religious education program similar to yours in my church and just wonderful things are happening."
>
> Colleen brightened. "Well, I'm pleased. I'm really excited to hear about that."
>
> He was dressed more informally than the others in a white shirt with an open collar and khaki-colored slacks. As Colleen turned to pick up a note pad, he said rather hurriedly, "I have to go now, but if you have time, I want to invite you to stop by our class. We meet early this evening."
>
> "I would love to," Colleen chirped and got the address.
>
> When the conference ended, Colleen hopped into a taxi and went to the address. She found herself in front of a huge building.

A massive stone church with an incredibly large bell tower was off to the left. The building in front of her, made of the same stone as the church, looked like an education building. Colleen was startled as the taxi drove off, leaving her in front of the intimidating structure just as darkness set in. She meekly approached the oak front doors. They were at least twelve feet high. She looked for a side door, but none was in sight. Colleen tried the large handle on the right door, and to her surprise, it opened.

Moving inside, she stopped dead in her tracks. She found herself in a long hallway with darkened classrooms on both sides. No one was in sight, but she could see light coming out of the last doorway on the right at the very end of the hall. Colleen made her way down the hall toward the light. Each footstep pierced the silence. She peeked through the open doors of the darkened classrooms as she passed. They all looked the same—a wooden podium in the front with desks lined up in rows of five all the way to the back of the room. It looked as though a hundred people could fit in each classroom, but the classrooms were all empty. The chalkboards in the classrooms were clean.

There were twelve classrooms on each side of the hallway. After getting halfway down the hall, Colleen looked back toward the front door. It had disappeared in the darkness. Her heart skipped a beat, and she ran the rest of the way toward the light. She slowed as she approached the end of the hallway and came to a stop just before the open door. Colleen peeked in and breathed a sigh of relief. The classroom was full of people of all descriptions. It was clearly an adult class, but there were young adults sitting on the floor in one corner, older adults in chairs in another corner, and groups of other adults in the middle. Colleen noticed that the back wall of the classroom was made of glass. She could see just as many people on the patio as there were inside. They also were in small groups, some in intense discussion, others laughing.

As her eyes adjusted to the light and activity, Colleen realized that music was playing in the patio area. She thought that no one noticed her, but then a man got up from one of the groups on the patio and waved. Colleen recognized the white shirt as he made his way to her.

"Hello, Colleen, welcome," he said.

Her face flushed, and she almost collapsed with relief. "You don't know how happy I am to be here," she replied. "I'm afraid that the hallway scared me a bit."

"Yes, we're trying to do something about that," he said. "We are just about ready to end our session. I'm happy that you came."

"It looks as if everyone is enjoying the class," Colleen replied. "You know that I forgot to ask you your name back at the conference."

He looked at her with a smile and said, "My name is Jesus."

I gasped and exclaimed, "Colleen, what a dream! What happened next?"

"I woke up," she said.

I couldn't help but ask her more about the dream. "Let me understand, it was Jesus who stopped by the booth back at the religious education conference?"

"Yes," she said.

"But no one else talked to you at the conference?"

"That's right," she replied.

"He not only talked to you, but he called you by name?"

"Yes," she said, her voice cracking with emotion.

"And he said that he was using your program?"

"Well, he said that he was using a program like mine," she said.

"Colleen, here was Jesus in the midst of all these people. Weren't they all just staring at him, transfixed by his presence?"

"No, he was in one of the small groups," she said.

We both paused, knowing the importance of the image. I continued. "All of the darkened classrooms were empty?"

"Yes, and very traditional looking," she replied.

"The classroom that Jesus was in was the same size as the rest?"

"Yes," she said. "But it seemed much more open, and remember there was a large patio outside."

"Colleen, what do you think this dream means?" I asked.

"I think we both know what it means," she replied.

We said our goodbyes.

I sat in silence for a long while. Then I turned to my computer and typed one line, "A Church at Risk."

# NOTES

## Chapter 1

1. All of the awakening stories are composites of events in the lives of real people. With the exception of my wife and myself, names and other details have been changed to protect the anonymity of everyone involved.

2. David W. Moore, "Most Americans Say Religion Is Important to Them," *The Gallup Organization Religion Poll Newsletter Archive* (February 1995).

3. Miriam Therese Winter, Adair Lummis, and Allison Stokes, *Defecting in Place* (New York: Crossroad, 1994). These authors use the term *defecting in place* to describe the alienation that women feel who embrace feminist values in a religious institutional setting. I use the term in a much broader sense.

4. *A Nation at Risk*, A Report to the Nation and the Secretary of Education United States Department of Education, The National Commission on Excellence in Education (April 1983).

## Chapter 2

1. Andrew Greeley, *Religious Change in America* (Cambridge, Mass.: Harvard University Press, 1989), 4–10.

2. For Greeley's analysis of the models and survey data, see *Religious Change in America*, 112–28.

3. Ibid., 90.

4. Ibid., 17; also see Robert Bezilla, ed., *Religion in America* (Princeton, N.J.: The Princeton Religion Research Center), 22.

5. Bezilla, *Religion in America*, 57.

6. Greeley, *Religious Change in America*, 115.

7. Ibid., 116; Bezilla, *Religion in America*, 43.

8. Greeley, *Religious Change in America*, 115; Bezilla, *Religion in America*, 10–11.

9. Greeley, *Religious Change in America*, 116–18.

10. Bezilla, *Religion in America*, 20.

11. Ibid., 12–13.

12. James Fowler, *Stages of Faith: The Psychology of Human Development and the Quest for Meaning* (San Francisco: Harper & Row, 1981).

13. Ibid., xii.

14. Ibid., 9–15. Fowler draws upon the work of Wilfred Cantwell Smith, a comparative-religion scholar, in describing these distinctions.

15. For a synopsis of a feminist critique of developmental research, see Carol Gilligan, "In a Different Voice: Visions of Maturity," in *Women's Spirituality*, ed. Joann W. Conn (Mahwah, N.J.: Paulist Press, 1986).

16. James Fowler, *Becoming Adult, Becoming Christian* (San Francisco: Harper & Row, 1984), 52–71. For a more comprehensive discussion of Fowler's stages see his *Stages of Faith.*

17. Fowler, *Stages of Faith,* 149.

18. For examples of civil or cultural religion, see Robert N. Bellah and Phillip E. Hammond, *Varieties of Civil Religion* (San Francisco: Harper & Row, 1980); Catherine L. Albanese, *America: Religions and Religion,* 2d ed. (Belmont, Calif.: Wadsworth, 1992).

19. Fowler, *Stages of Faith,* 179.

20. Ibid., 198.

21. Ibid., 201.

22. George Gallup, Jr., and Jim Castelli, *The People's Religion* (New York: Macmillan, 1989), 20–21.

23. Fowler, *Becoming Adult, Becoming Christian,* 95.

24. Fowler, *Stages of Faith,* 103–5.

## Chapter 3

1. Elements of these tele-evangelist stories are fictitious, but the thrust of the stories is representative of fundamentalist tele-evangelism.

2. Martin Marty and R. Scott Appleby, *The Glory and the Power* (Boston: Beacon Press, 1992), 16.

3. Bruce B. Lawrence, *Defenders of God* (San Francisco: Harper & Row, 1989), 8–17.

4. Ibid., 9.

5. Ibid., 11.

6. I rely upon Nancy T. Ammerman's analysis of modernist thought as expressed in Martin Marty and R. Scott Appleby, eds., *Fundamentalisms Observed* (Chicago: University of Chicago Press, 1991), 8–13.

7. Ibid., 11.

8. Ibid., 12.

9. Ibid., vii.

10. Lawrence, *Defenders of God,* 27.

11. I follow Nancy T. Ammerman's analysis of U.S. Protestant fundamentalist history expressed in "North American Protestant Fundamentalism," in Marty and Appleby, *Fundamentalisms Observed,* chap. 1.

12. Ibid., 2.

13. Ibid., 16.

14. Lawrence, *Defenders of God,* 182–84.

15. Marty and Appleby, *The Glory and the Power,* 37–45.

16. William Dinges, "Roman Catholic Traditionalism," in Marty and Appleby, *Fundamentalisms Observed,* 66–101.

17. Ibid., 78.

18. Andrew Greeley, *Religious Change in America* (Cambridge, Mass.: Harvard University Press, 1989).

19. Marty and Appleby, *The Glory and the Power,* 34. For more on fundamentalism, see their other recent works, which include *Fundamentalisms Observed; Fundamentalisms and Society* (Chicago: University of

Chicago Press, 1993); and *Fundamentalisms and the State* (Chicago: University of Chicago Press, 1993).

20. Ibid., 10–34.

21. Charles B. Strozier, *Apocalypse: On a Psychology of Fundamentalism* (Boston: Beacon Press, 1994), 1–3.

22. H. Richard Niebuhr, *Christ and Culture* (New York: Harper & Row, 1956).

## Chapter 4

1. For a good discussion about Christian moral decision-making, see Richard Gula, *What Are They Saying About Moral Norms?* (New York: Paulist Press, 1982).

2. See Bernard Lee, *The Future Church of 140 BCE* (New York: Crossroad, 1996) for a discussion of communal power.

3. Thomas Berry and Brian Swimme give excellent introductions to this notion of a sacred universe. See Thomas Berry, *The Dream of the Earth* (San Francisco: Sierra Club Books, 1988); Brian Swimme and Thomas Berry, *The Universe Story* (San Francisco: HarperCollins, 1994).

## Chapter 5

1. Bernard Bailyn, *Education in the Forming of American Society* (New York: Vintage, 1960).

2. Gabriel Moran, *Religious Education as a Second Language* (Birmingham, Ala.: Religious Education Press, 1989), 39–40.

3. Lawrence Cremin, *Traditions of American Education* (New York: Basic Books, 1977), 108.

4. Lawrence Cremin, *Public Education* (New York: Basic Books, 1976), 27.

5. Ibid., 27–38.

6. Mortimer J. Adler, *The Paideia Proposal: An Educational Manifesto* (New York: Macmillan, 1982).

7. George Bernard Shaw, *Man and Superman: A Comedy and a Philosophy* (Westminster: Archebald Constable & Co., 1903).

8. John Dewey, "My Pedagogic Creed," *The School Journal* 54, 3 (January 16, 1897), reprinted in Howard A. Ozmon and Samuel M. Craver, *Philosophical Foundations of Education*, 3d ed. (Columbus, Ohio: Merrill Publishing, 1987), 123–26.

9. Ibid., 119.

10. Thomas S. Kuhn, *The Structure of Scientific Revolutions*, in *International Encyclopedia of Unified Science* 2(2) (Chicago: University of Chicago Press, 1970).

11. Kurt Lewin, *Field Theory in Social Science* (New York: Harper & Row, 1951), 169.

12. John Dewey, *Experience and Education* (New York: Macmillan, 1963), reprint of the 1938 Kappa Delta Pi edition.

13. Cremin, *Public Education*, 19.

14. John Dewey, *Democracy and Education* (New York: Free Press, 1916).

15. Richard J. Bernstein, *Philosophical Profiles: Essays in the Pragmatic Mode* (Philadelphia: University of Pennsylvania Press, 1986), 261.

16. Ibid., 269–70.

17. See Jack Seymour, Robert T. O'Gorman, and Charles R. Foster, *The Church in the Education of the Public* (Nashville: Abingdon Press, 1984) for a good history of how Christian churches have participated in the education of the American people and a call for a reconceptualization of the practice of religious education.

## Chapter 6

1. Bernard J. F. Lonergan, *Collection* (New York: Herder & Herder, 1967), 232–33.

2. Bernard J. F. Lonergan, *Method in Theology* (New York: Herder & Herder, 1972), 57.

3. F. E. Crowe, *Old Things and New: A Strategy for Education*, a supplementary issue of the *Lonergan Workshop* journal, vol. 5 (Atlanta, Ga.: Scholars Press, 1985).

4. Lonergan, *Collection*, 224.

5. Lonergan, *Method in Theology*, 3–25.

6. Ibid., 20–24.

7. Ibid., 35.

8. Bernard J. F. Lonergan, *Insight: A Study of Human Understanding* (New York: Harper & Row, 1978), 218–42; original work published New York: Longman Group Publications, 1957.

9. Ibid., 225.

10. Lonergan, *Method in Theology*, 235–45.

11. Walter E. Conn, "The Desire for Authenticity," in Vernon Gregson, ed., *The Desires of the Human Heart* (Mahwah, N.J.: Paulist Press, 1988), 53.

12. Lonergan, *Method in Theology*, 242.

13. Robert M. Doran, "Introduction to Lonergan: An Appreciation," in Gregson, *The Desires of the Human Heart*, 8–11.

14. Lonergan, *Insight: A Study of Human Understanding*, 225–42.

15. Lonergan, *Method in Theology*, 43–81.

16. Lawrence Cremin, *Public Education* (New York: Basic Books, 1976), 77.

17. Kurt Lewin, *Field Theory in Social Science* (New York: Harper & Row, 1951), 169.

18. Clark Kerr, *The Uses of the University* (Cambridge: Harvard University Press, 1963).

19. Alfred North Whitehead, *The Aims of Education* (New York: Macmillan, 1929), 14.

20. Parker Palmer, *To Know As We Are Known: A Spirituality of Education* (San Francisco: Harper & Row, 1983), 17–20.

## Chapter 7

1. S. L. Albrecht and T. B. Heaton, "Secularization, Education, and Religiosity," *Review of Religious Research* 26(1) (1984), 43–58.

2. Robert Bezilla, ed., *Religion in America, 1992–93* (Princeton, N.J.: Princeton Religion Research Center, 1991), 59–61.

3. George M. Marsden and Bradley J. Longfield, eds., *The Secularization of the Academy* (New York: Oxford University Press, 1992), 9.

4. Douglas A. Sloan, "The Higher Learning and Social Vision," *Teachers College Record* 79(2), 163–69. Sloan's historical and epistemological analysis is used throughout this section.

5. Bradley J. Longfield, "From Evangelicalism to Liberalism: Public Midwestern Universities in Nineteenth-Century America," in Marsden and Longfield, *The Secularization of the Academy*, 46–73.

6. Douglas A. Sloan, *Insight-Imagination: The Emancipation of Thought and the Modern World* (Westport, Conn.: Greenwood, 1983), x-9.

7. Ibid., 10.

8. Ibid., xiii.

9. Robert Bellah, "The New Religious Consciousness and the Secular University," *Daedalus* 1 (1974), 110–15.

10. G. R. Bucher, *The Study of Religion in Church-Related Higher Education: A Report* (Sherman, Tex.: Austin College Center for Program and Institutional Renewal, 1980).

11. Kaasa, Harris, et al., *Humanism: A Christian Perspective* (Collegeville, Minn.: St. John's University, 1981) (ERIC Document Reproduction Service No. ED 213 275).

12. M. R. Berquist and T. E. Dillon, "The Great-Books Curriculum at a Reforming Catholic College," *The Journal of General Education* 32(2) (Spring 1980), 123–34.

13. E. J. Power, *A History of Catholic Higher Education in the United States* (Milwaukee: Bruce, 1958).

14. Phillip Gleason, "American Catholic Higher Education: A Historical Perspective," in R. Hassenger, ed., *The Shape of Catholic Higher Education* (Chicago: University of Chicago Press, 1967), 15–53.

15. Ibid., 45.

16. Robert T. O'Gorman, *The Church That Was a School: Catholic Identity and Catholic Education in the United States Since 1790*, a monograph on the history of Catholic Education in the United States written for the Catholic Education Futures Project (Washington, D.C.: National Catholic Education Association, 1987), 9.

17. R. Hassenger, "The Structure of Catholic Higher Education," in P. Gleason, ed., *Contemporary Catholicism in the United States* (Notre Dame, Ind.: University of Notre Dame Press, 1969), 295–323.

18. Ibid., 323.

19. John Elias, "Catholic Philosophy of Education," paper presented at the annual meeting of the Association of Professors and Researchers in Religious Education, Chicago, Ill. (October 1988).

20. Ibid., 7.

21. Ibid., 9.

22. Ibid., 13.

23. Ibid., 14.

24. Fayette B. Veverka, "For God and Country: Catholic Schooling in the 1920's." *Dissertation Abstracts International* 45(2) (1984), 436–37.

25. M. T. Moeser, F. J. Buckley, J. A. Grau, W. J. Shea, and P. Surlis, "Preliminary Report of the CTS Committee on Profession of Faith/Oath of Fidelity," *Horizons* 17 (1990), 103–27.

26. See M. J. Adler, *The Paideia Proposal: An Educational Manifesto* (New York: Macmillan, 1982); idem, *Reforming Education: The Opening of the American Mind* [a collection of Adler works], ed. Geraldine Van Doren (New York: Macmillan, 1988); A. Bloom, *The Closing of the American Mind* (New York: Simon and Schuster, 1987); P. Smith, *Killing the Spirit: Higher Education in America* (New York: Viking, 1990).

27. Douglas A. Sloan, "The Higher Learning and Social Vision," *Teachers College Record* 79(2) (1977), 163–69.

28. B. P. Hall, *The Development of Consciousness* (New York: Paulist Press, 1976), 2–3.

29. For a good sense of Thomas Berry's thought on the environment, see Thomas Berry, *The Dream of the Earth* (San Francisco: Sierra Club Books, 1988) and Brian Swimme and Thomas Berry, *The Universe Story* (San Francisco: HarperSanFrancisco, 1992).

30. Lonergan, *Method in Theology*, 79.

31. Lawrence Cremin, *Public Education* (New York: Basic Books, 1977), 57–77.

32. Ibid., 72.

33. Ibid., 75.

34. J. S. Brubacker, *On the Philosophy of Higher Education* (San Francisco: Jossey-Bass, 1977), 116–23.

35. Ibid., 116.

36. Alfred McBride, "The Value Neutral Catholic College," *Momentum* 11(2) (1980), 28–34.

37. Ibid., 33.

38. Ibid., 34.

39. L. Orsy, *The Church: Learning and Teaching* (Wilmington, Del.: Michael Glazier, 1987), 110–13.

40. Ibid., 111.

41. Ibid., 110.

42. Ibid., 130.

43. G. Davis, *Should the Church-Related College Religion Professor Enjoy the Right of Academic Freedom?*, American Association of University Professors (1983) (ERIC Document Reproduction service No. ED 226 678).

44. Ibid., 9.

45. Martin Marty, "Future Church-Culture Relations and Their Impact on Church-Related Higher Education—The Student Nexus," *Liberal Education* 64(4) (1978), 383–401.

46. J. Ortega y Gasset, *Mission of the University* (New York: W. W. Norton, 1944).

47. A primary thrust of Sloan's *Insight-Imagination* is his call for the formulation of an epistemological radicalism that counters the positivistic orthodoxy of value-free knowledge.

48. Bernard J. F. Lonergan, *The Philosophy of Catholic Education*, unpublished manuscript. This is a transcription of lectures given by Lonergan

in 1959 and edited by J. Quinn and J. Quinn (available from the Lonergan Research Center, Regis College, Toronto, Ontario, Canada, 1979), 30–97.

### Chapter 8

1. Phyllis A. Tickle, *Re-discovering the Sacred: Spirituality in America* (New York: Crossroad, 1995).

2. Jim Castelli and Joseph Gremillion, *The Emerging Parish: The Notre Dame Study of Catholic Life Since Vatican II* (San Francisco: Harper & Row, 1987), 3–4. Also see Philip J. Murnion, *New Parish Ministers: Laity and Religious on Parish Staffs* (New York: The National Pastoral Life Center, 1992), v.

3. David Tracy, *Plurality and Ambiguity* (San Francisco: Harper & Row, 1987).

4. See Robert Ludwig, *Reconstructing Catholicism* (New York: Crossroad, 1995) for a contemporary articulation of salvation as relationship.

5. Alfred North Whitehead, *The Aims of Education* (New York: Macmillan, 1929), 25.

6. Gabriel Moran, *Interplay* (Winona, Minn.: Saint Mary's Press, Christian Brothers Publications, 1981).

7. Avery Dulles, S.J., *Models of the Church* (New York: Image Books, 1978).

8. H. Richard Niebuhr, *Christ and Culture* (New York: Harper & Row, 1951).

9. John M. Staudenmaier, S.J., "Technology—Reading the Signs of the Times," *Conversations* 9 (Spring 1996), 5–11.

10. Thomas Berry spoke about earth life systems as the context for human health and culture in a series of lectures presented at Loyola University New Orleans in the spring semester of 1996.

11. Timothy Casey, "Philosophy of Technology in the Jesuit University," *Conversations* 9 (Spring 1996), 19.

12. Paul Soukup, S.J., "Invisible, Inevitable, Paradoxical Technology," *Conversations* 9 (Spring 1996), 23–27.

13. See Bernard Cook's insightful analysis in *The Distancing of God* (Minneapolis: Fortress Press, 1990).